8 KEYS: A SPECIAL DELIVERY MESSAGE FROM THE ANGELS

By

Linda West

With

Karen Miller Gibbs

Illustration ©Journeymakers, Inc. by Lynda Louise Mangoro

8 Keys: A Special Delivery Message From The Angels

By Linda West with Karen Miller Gibbs

Journeymakers, Inc. Publishing - www.voiceoftheangels.com

©2010 Linda West and Karen Miller Gibbs

Published in the United States of America by special
arrangement with Linda West and Karen Miller Gibbs

The information contained in this book is intended for educational
purposes only. It is not a substitute or replacement for medical advice
or counseling offered by licensed health care providers, or to be used
for medical diagnosis or treatment. It is not the intent of the authors or
publisher of this book to give medical advice or engage in the practice
of medicine and they are held harmless for any misuse of the material
by the reader.

Cover art by Rebecca Hayes

ISBN 13: 978-0-9841142-3-8

Printed in the United States of America

The power of even one of these keys by itself is amazing. Put all eight together and you have a wealth of timely, integrative information that is capable of completely changing your life and moving you forward in positive directions as never before. Interwoven throughout the book and Linda's personal story are special meditations. When you put everything together you have a fundamental foundation for great and profound change. Here, Linda West has successfully combined and integrated the physical with the metaphysical. Within these pages you will discover that she has made manifest in her own life the creation of the kingdom of heaven on Earth, which is exactly what the angels are teaching us all to do here. This book is a brilliant and quintessential blueprint.
– Dyan Garris, visionary mystic, New Age musician and author of *Money and Manifesting*

The wonderful messages in Linda West's book "8 Keys: A Special Delivery Message from the Angels" are clearly from the Angels and God. In fact, she concludes with the Eighth Key, "Connection," which contains mainly "I Am" statements. This sums up that everything is connected, especially to God, All There Is, Was, and Ever Shall Be. Linda, through many of her own personal experiences, sets the stage for each "key" or principle. These principles, if taken to heart and applied by the reader, have the power to transform one's life. The information set forth is a catalyst that helps free one from psychic pain and any negative past experiences/ encounters still held onto by the mental and emotional portions of one's being. The book is a guide to a life full of joy and happiness. – Elliott Eli Jackson, author of *From God to You: Absolute Truth*

"The beautiful and inspiring message in '8 Keys' lifted me up so high that the only word to express it is: AWESOME! And it gives me so much comfort to know that we are surrounded and loved by our wonderful angels, and that they are *always* with us."
– Joyce, Phoenix, AZ

"Reading the '8 Keys,' I felt such a personal connection to Linda and her raw and very real emotion. The courage it took to share is more than amazing. It is a treasured gift. Because of her personal touches, the lessons have a beautiful simplicity that allow you to engage yourself in the principles of the 8 Keys and, most importantly, apply them, remember them, and study them with ease. The entire book left me with incredible tools, and an understanding of how to apply them in my life."
– Em Miller, Shelton, WA

"'8 Keys' is a pithy, sharp, spiritually enlightening book, extremely well written and a joy to read! Thank you for this book!!!"
– Nikki, Las Vegas, NV

"'8 Keys' is a beautiful and inspiring message of hope, with examples of real life challenges and how to overcome them."
– E. J. F., Cave Creek, AZ

"I lent your book to my sister to read, but her husband read it first and it has really affected him. He now relates a Key to everything. He has them memorized and recites them like a prophet! He is a changed man and credits the '8 Keys' for it!"
– N. A. Dougherty, Nevada

"Linda's book, '8 Keys: A Special Delivery Message from the Angels' has changed my life. It has given me the tools to free my life of the negative energy that has surrounded me most of my life. Using the eight Keys and reading how Linda was able to change her life, gave me the courage and the know-how, to change mine! I recommend this book to anyone who doesn't know how they got where they are, but want to get out of the mess their life has become!" – K.G., Cave Creek, AZ

"I always felt that there were angels surrounding me and now I know it! This book has helped me to be aware that my angels are always looking out for me and leading me to the healing and enlightenment I need. Thank you, Linda and Karen, for bringing the '8 Keys' into my life!" – J.M., Phoenix, AZ

"I felt as if Linda had written the book for me, like it was my life story she was writing about. Every night I read one chapter to absorb its message. And I am filled with such a peaceful, calming energy. She gives me hope to overcome my own childhood. It's amazing how open and frank she is about her abuse. She doesn't hold anything back. It's right in the open for everyone to read about. I've bought several copies for my children and friends." – Veda, Alpine, Arizona

INTRODUCTION

Linda West is a psychic medium with a Master's Degree in Metaphysics. She is a certified Angel Therapy Practitioner® and Theta Healer, a licensed massage therapist, and a certified Biofeedback technician. Her practice currently consists of angel readings, massage therapy, and Quantum Energy Medicine with SCIO (the Scientific Consciousness Interface Operations). As a metaphysician, Ms. West combines the work of a teacher, psychologist, and spiritual healer/counselor by using applied psychology and universal spiritual truths, as well as connecting with her angels and those of her clients.

She believes that it is important to bring to you this message that lets you know that you can have perfect health, perfect wealth, perfect love, and perfect self expression. She brings this message to you to help you connect with your spirituality, to help you find out that God and your angels want you to be happy, and to help you see that you are worthy and special, that happiness and abundance are what you deserve.

In this book, Linda offers you the opportunity to learn how to open yourself to the higher frequencies of energy that help you heal and grow in enlightenment. As you read and study this book, you will learn to recognize the sound of the voices of the angels, and learn what God wants you to know about Him/Her and yourself. You will be given the tools to embrace your life and become everything you never expected you could become, but always wanted to be. You will learn how to avoid the pitfalls that keep you from reaping the benefit of your connection to the infinite source of all good in the universe.

This book was written especially for each of you who are searching for your path but who may be having difficulty finding it, to help you connect with your angels, and most of all, to help you find the answer to the questions: *Who am I? And why am I here?*

CONTENTS

A Personal Message from Linda West

The information regarding the "Eight Keys to the Kingdom" was given to me during live, audio taped presentations. Those portions of this book relating to the Keys were based on the information on those tapes. The information has been edited to make reading easier, and to include more that the angels wanted you to have. Although I tried to prepare myself for each presentation, to at least make an outline in my head, it became clear to me that the angels wanted to have their say. Time after time I found my mental outline pushed aside and the information from the angels coming spontaneously. I tried many times during those live presentations to bring myself back to my outline. But each time the angels would have their way, not mine!

If you are new to the subject of metaphysics, you will want to take what you think you know, or what you think you believe, and put it aside for now. Pay particular attention to anything you read in this book that makes you angry or upset, or any part that you want to skip because it makes you feel too uncomfortable. That anger or discomfort is what the angels want you to feel, because they want you to pay most attention to those points. Whatever has pushed your buttons is exactly the issue you need to work on. So pay close attention to how those issues make you feel.

I understand that many of you won't believe everything I tell you has come from the angels, or even that there are angels. That is perfectly fine with me, because it is not my intention to change your mind about what or in whom you believe. But I am here to help you open up your heart to see things, maybe in another dimension. Whether you accept what I say or you don't really isn't the important thing. What is important is that you digest it, that you take it into your heart and in the end say, "I'm more confident in what I believe now than I was yesterday.

So I present to you this message from the angels. And it is my profound belief that as intended by God and the Angels, this message is going to change your life.

P.S. In the time that has passed since this message from the angels was first presented to me, once again, I find that the angels will have their way! After the first printing of this book, so much has come to light about the rising of the Goddess in the Earth during this time that the angels with whom I communicate feel it important to reflect now upon the changes that have resulted. One major change that they insist upon is in reference to the perception we have about our Source, whom we call "God." I still call that source God. But contrary to the images most of us grew up with of a male persona – Father God – the image that the angels have shaped in my mind, and the one that they want to share with you is much more amorphous, having no gender and no particular shape but definitely demonstrates the softer, more nurturing nature of a female.

The stereotypes we know of as male energy – using physical strength and political/economical power in order to bring about change and to rule in the world – are giving way to those characteristics we most often associate with female energy, i.e., intuition, spirituality, and empowerment by healing and nurturing.

Science has shown us that all humans are first conceived as females, and males develop from that form. Because all human conception has the possibility of becoming male or remaining female, this duality of nature remains within us throughout our lives We each retain the essence of our opposite, which waxes and wanes along our lifeline, and is allowing us now to be affected by the rising power of the Goddess. That Goddess dwells within each of us, male and female alike.

Whether you are a male reader or a female, your female characteristics will become stronger with the rising Goddess. This does not mean that males will become female, or that any of us will reflect more or less of the gender we are. But accepting that we are both female AND male will help us to understand and benefit from the changes that are taking shape in the world.

This means that struggling against change will be less effective than understanding and working with the changes. That "powering" through your difficulties will not bring you the end results you expect, and it is more likely that persistent pursuit of your goals will bring you success more effectively than aggressive pursuit. By embracing patience, perseverance, and a willingness to welcome the Goddess within you, you will find the path to your goals made much easier.

One of the most effective ways to begin to work with these changes is to relax our need to identify with our Divine Source in a specific gender form and to change the descriptive words we attach to it. So in this edition I have changed, wherever possible, the words

I use to give name to this Source in order to help you free yourself from the images that limit your acceptance, so that you may if you so choose, wander into the possibilities offered by a God who is everything and withholds nothing from you.

With these thoughts in mind, please accept this offering from the angels for the gift it is. Feel free to entertain the thought of the presence of angels in your life – starting now. – Linda West

A Note from Karen Miller Gibbs

Most people who meet Linda West see a woman whose humor, exuberantly outgoing energy, and vivacious beauty defy anyone's perception of middle-age. They see a confident, successful business woman and inspiring motivational speaker. They see an enthusiastic proponent of metaphysics and natural foods and remedies, and a tireless therapist and counselor to hundreds of clients.

What I learned of Linda over months of pouring through her diary-like notes and countless hours of interviews and listening to her voice on tape is that this extraordinary woman is as down to earth and "ordinary" as any of the working people/parents you may know, or as you, yourself, may be.

What is strikingly different about her is her willingness to put her vulnerabilities out on the table for anyone to see and to share the lessons of the "8 Keys" that she has learned on her way to wholeness.

Linda's courage goes beyond the offering of her private fears and struggles for public scrutiny. She also has no qualms about admitting that she hears voices in her head – the voices of angels! In Linda's seminars she has a way of putting forth her knowledge of metaphysics and the wisdom she receives from the angels in a straightforward, easy to understand and easy to apply style. In this book we've tried to use that easy style to tell the poignant story of this very ordinary woman who, through extraordinary experiences, learned the wisdom of the "8 Keys" the hard way. Linda shows us that ordinary people can overcome any adversity and grow in spirituality and enlightenment. I have come to believe that if Linda can do it, anyone can!

From the introduction to the epilogue, in 8 Keys – A Special Delivery Message from the Angels, Linda, the angels, and I have tried to take you on a remarkable journey from "believing to connecting," from fear to freedom, and provide you with the tools you will need for your own journey to spiritual enlightenment. We hope this will be the book that will be too precious to lend and that you will make a gift of a second book to a friend in need of its wisdom.

The driving force behind this book is to show you that through the wisdom of the "Keys," you can take responsibility for your actions, create self-awareness and empower yourself to guide your own destiny. Linda did, and you can too. – Karen Miller Gibbs

Prologue: One Summer for the Angels

I was a little nervous on a Sunday morning in June of 2006. I was on my way to deliver my first presentation of the "Eight Keys to the Kingdom" to the little church near my home in the White Mountains of eastern Arizona. Having been a public speaker for many years, I am not usually nervous before I do a presentation or seminar. But that morning was very different. I had been involved the week just past in an alternative health expo where I gave two seminars and didn't have time to prepare for the presentation to the church. I protested to the angels, "You know, I don't even have an outline in my head!"

And they said, "All the information is going to come through. Don't worry about it."

So being the normal, secure human being I have always been, I started to worry! But the angels just kept reassuring me. As I returned to my efforts to outline the points for my presentation, thoughts began jumping into my head, like remembering that I had left a friend's extension cord at the expo. More random thoughts followed, one after the other, each compelling enough to warrant my consideration and to grab my complete attention. It became obvious the angels didn't want me to have any preparation for that morning's talk.

Just as I pulled into the parking lot of the church my cell phone rang. I answered and heard this strained little voice say, "Mom?"

"Jessie? Jessie, is that you?" And she just started crying.

"Honey, what's the matter?"

My husband, Scott, bless his heart, thought he was doing me a favor when he asked our daughter to call me as a surprise. He thought it might take some of the stress out of my day. Jessica, our only child, was fifteen-years old and away from home for the first time. She was taking an opportunity offered through her school, to live with a family in Germany for a month, and it had been a couple of days since we had heard from her,

"Nothing," she said, not trying to be brave at all.

Why do kids always tell you "nothing" when you know darn well there is "something?"

"No, no. You're calling me from Germany! Is the host family okay? Is everything alright there? Are you doing alright?"

"Yes," she said sniffling back tears. My heart was racing with the kind of panic only a parent separated from their only child by an ocean and several land masses could feel. Now I was not only anxious about the presentation, I was completely undone by concern for my absent child!

Thank you, Scott! And, by the way, thank you angels! Once again, my thoughts were captured and held, overwhelmingly, so that I could not possibly think what I might say in that morning's presentation.

As it turned out Jessie was very, very homesick. What do you say when you're half way across the world from someone you love so much who needs you right now? I did the only thing I could do – the thing that has taken me so many years to learn – I asked God to take care of her and to handle my anxiety. And then I sent her angels.

That's what I do. I rely on God and I communicate with angels. I speak "Angel," and I do Angel Readings. It's a promise I made years ago to God. I didn't always speak Angel. It took a lot of work and many years of healing before I was well enough and strong enough to trust God enough to live in the moment...enough so that I could hear the angels.

My prayers for Jessie worked pretty well because she called a few days later happy and excited to tell me what incredible shopping there was in Europe, and it was a shame that I was missing it! And (Oh, yeah), would I please put more money in her account? Kids. Gotta love 'em!

As I began the presentation that morning, I said another prayer, this time for me. I took a deep breath, relaxed my shoulders, opened wide all my chakras, and invited the angels to speak. The words, the basis for this book, jumped into my head and started to pour out. Regardless of the lack of my own preparation, as always, the angels came through.

Although I speak Angel, I am not slighting anyone else who's on the other side. I have learned that we all don't call the Power that is in charge of this universe by the same name. In the context of my life it has been known as God, Jesus, the angels, the Universe, Mother Nature, Mother God, Father God, Spirit, and many more. Regardless of the name we each give this power it is all the same energy. And that energy is Love. However, that energy has identified itself to me as angels. So I speak Angel. I leave it to you to use your own term for the Infinite Love Energy that rules the universe and with whom you wish to communicate.

Each of you reading this now is being communicated to by angels. Everything about this book is because of the angels. I am a medium, a psychic, a healer, and the angels have given a message for you through me, and they have guided me to the people who have helped me get the information to you. Who am I to be their messenger? I am a rather ordinary human with all the same issues that many of you have had to face and some, I pray, most of you will never have to encounter. My life has been full of errors, and searching, and rejecting, and unforgiveness, and stubbornness, and habits to overcome. I am full of scars, as each of us is, as we weather circumstances and stumble over, around, and through our lives.

It took me a while, but I finally learned not to question the angels whether I am "good" enough or "special" enough to receive messages and guidance from them. That is the primary point the angels want you to know. No one needs to be "special," "good," or "worthy." Each of us can learn to speak to and listen to angels. Each of us is loved, without conditions, so completely by that Infinite Love Energy that it wants to communicate with us at any moment we are willing to listen.

This message comes to you from those who want you to love all your scars, who want you to understand that those scars made you who you are. It comes from those who want you to understand that those scars may very well be the reason you chose to come to this planet. Part of the angels' message that came to me that summer was that I am to tell you of my scars. So this book is really two things: the "Eight Keys to the Kingdom," and bits of the story of my journey in this life. I hope you find relevance in the connections between those bits and the angels' message. I hope you begin to truly understand how your life and the angels are connected, how you and I are connected, and why the message of the "Eight Keys to the Kingdom" is important to us both.

We have laid out each chapter in such a way that you can choose to read the whole thing, only the section on the Keys, or perhaps only those sections that came from my life. As in all of life, the choice is yours. Take from this work that which will most benefit and enhance your own work and life.

How the "Eight Keys to the Kingdom" Came To Be

The summer of 2006 was to be a special time on our mountain, according to the angels. I felt a restlessness that comes from impending change in my life. So I was not surprised one morning when the angels woke me around three o'clock. According to many authorities in metaphysics, the most profound decisions are made and the most amazing information is received between one and three in the morning. That morning, the angels told me that I was to prepare to tell people about eight keys.

"What keys," I thought?

"To the Kingdom," they answered. "Tell them about the Eight Keys to the Kingdom."

They said I should make a series of the Eight Keys, and that they would give me the information about each one. I knew that would be a lot of information and I would have to write it down. I don't much like to write. The angels know this of me. But I knew there would be so much information that I would have to write it down. As I prepared to receive the information, I thought, "Oh boy. This is going to take forever." And I was more than a little grumpy about it.

You see, my deal with the angels for speaking on their behalf, and I do it often, was that it would be easy. I own two businesses and my husband owns another. And then there was this certain fifteen-year old going on twenty-five, if you know what I mean. Time was and is a very valuable commodity. I just knew it would take a very large chunk of my time to sit and write down all that information about those Keys.

It took about twenty minutes. I was amazed, although I don't know why, because the angels always keep their promises. But as I sat there writing, I was puzzled because I only got a list of eight single words. I asked the angels, "What's this? What am I supposed to do with this?" Of course the answer was simple. The message is the point. Each of these eight words, each Key, is what makes the message work.

Not being one to argue with divine inspiration, I said, "Okay, but a lot of details and definitions are going to be repeated for many of these different Keys!" And the angels said, "Well, you understand, humans can be very thick. Sometimes they need to be told over and over. But it's all divine. And you know divine is always simple."

From that list of eight words came a series of eight presentations delivered over sixteen weeks. From that series, came this book. During my studies to become an Angel Therapist®, I learned that the angels communicate with us many times through numbers. According to Dr. Doreen Virtue, Ph.D. in her books Angels 101 and Angel Numbers, the number 300 means that (and I paraphrase): God and the ascended masters are present, the connection is clear and pure, and they are communicating with you.

In other words: "Listen up, Mortal. We have something we want you to hear!"

So go get your favorite hot or frosty beverage, snuggle down in your most comfortable reading chair, and take a journey with us as we present to you this very special message of the 8 Keys, sent to you from the angels. And if you have the inclination, read a little about how those angels came into my life.

Linda's Story: I Gotta Do What I Gotta Do

July 5, 1954, Elvis Presley recorded "That's Alright Mama," and at approximately 10:35 A.M. I was born. There was only one problem. My mother was not a bit happy with the whole pregnancy/motherhood thing. There was already one little girl at home, brought into the world by people totally unprepared to be parents. And here I came ready to offer them a whole new set of challenges.

My mom, a daughter of immigrants, raised in a home steeped in a set of old world values, was one of many women of her time who didn't feel they had a lot of say in their future. The women's liberation movement was still more than a decade away and there were little to no cultural examples to give these young women any idea that they could do more than their own mothers had done to secure their futures: marry and have babies. No one in my mom's family had much education at the time, and school was not an option for her either. To make life even more difficult, her family was particularly dysfunctional and very unhappy. When my father came into my mother's life, she jumped at the chance to escape that unhappiness by marrying him.

Of course, we don't really escape our families and the effects of the parenting we received, without truly understanding what it is we are escaping from and to. But we think being away from it is better. Mom didn't know that she would jump from that dysfunctional situation only to create a near duplicate, that she would choose a man so like her father. Like us all, she was just continuing to do what was comfortable and familiar to her. But that new dysfunctional situation was what I was born into, and have come to affectionately call my family.

It's been a really interesting life so far, filled with a lot of opportunities to advance in enlightenment and to learn from my mistakes. One of the things I learned somewhere along my journey, is that we pick our parents and the situations we are born into depending upon what we choose to accomplish in any given lifetime. And that has helped me to better understand and profit from this life. But before I go further, let me explain what I mean. There are better sources of explanation than this book, so I will just give you the gist of it, by using a metaphor of the "Big Bang" to attempt to explain what could be to some, a very complicated concept.

In the beginning there was just energy, the Divine Energy we call God. That energy wanted to know itself in a different way, so...the Big Bang. That "bang" was God taking billions of pieces of Him/Herself, purposefully creating an explosion of souls, such as we know on Earth, from those pieces. These souls, at their own discretion, take on various lives and forms, choosing to live in various planes, or worlds, realms, and dimensions. We souls on earth have experienced life in many of these planes. Many of us have had thousands of lives, each time refining our souls, hopefully working toward more enlightenment. In this way, God gets to know Himself through our experiences. Thus, the declaration "We are all one." And the admonition to "become one with the universe," makes a little more sense, since we all have the "One" energy flowing within us.

Each of us is God incarnate having an experience in a physical body. We, as humans, have a great deal of power because we are this God source. But few of us know what to do with this power or even understand what it means. This is the primary purpose of having multiple lifetimes. There is too much to learn about this power and what we are to do with it for one go-around. It may take one whole life span to learn just one small point. Along the way we make grand errors that become baggage in our future lives.

Looking at human history in general, some of our past lives have been pretty horrendous. Look at the way we have treated each other over the centuries, killing one another for religion, power, land, money, fame, and "just because." We have done this to ourselves, for we are our own ancestors. Our souls occupied those tyrannized and tortured great-grand relatives.

I have discovered over the years that many of my own past lives were spent exploring the spiritual. My soul has spent time in Lemuria and Atlantis. I have had dreams, meditations, and memories that verify this to me. I don't spend much time questioning this. But what I have read and studied validates what I know to be true for myself. The Bible promises us, "Ask and it shall be given; Seek and ye shall find." I have found this to be absolutely true. God, the angels, the universe, that Love Energy, will always give you the validation you need. The trick is to be paying attention, to notice when you are being validated. Too often it's written off as a coincidence. Sorry, there is no such thing as coincidence.

When I work with clients I try not to spend too much time on past lives, unless it has a direct effect on what is going on in this life. We can get carried away trying to figure out if we were Cleopatra or Marc Antony. Often though, past lives can have an impact on how we react to things now. For me, the dreams and memories of being burned at the stake, imprisoned, beheaded, and generally not well liked for my spiritual connections, had been a dominant factor for hiding my spirituality, which is the very essence of who I am.

I have spent many lives working with herbs, the earth, and healing. I was a sorceress, a healer, a seer. I knew how to work with the spiritual powers of light to help others. Not all my lives have been filled with love and light. But the lives that impact this life have had a spiritual connection. In each of those lives, just as in this one, I have been psychic, intuitive, whatever you choose to call it, and my spiritual connection has been very potent. However, in this go-round, I didn't always know that. I came into the knowledge from an unexpected direction.

Early in my teen years I became good friends with a pastor's daughter and I was invited to go to her church, which was a charismatic Pentecostal denomination. I am sure you know the kind: singing, clapping, crying hallelujah, speaking in tongues, and of course, "Thank ya, Jesus!!!!" I am not making fun here. I took all this very seriously and still do. Jesus is a great friend of mine and I have always felt His spirit very close to me. This was my first experience with organized religion and I embraced it with vigor. "Jesus Saves," became my mantra and I made sure everyone knew it. I studied the Bible feverishly and I knew all the songs in the church hymnal. Speaking in tongues was commonplace for me, and of course, I could do interpretations of those tongues. I was involved with all aspects and was thoroughly enamored with the whole process.

The church setting filled a need in my soul. I helped others who were lost find their way. I was a good girl. And for every saved soul I could see the jewels adding up in my heavenly crown. And boy was I just racking them up! All was well and good except...I began to wonder what happened to all the people around the world that didn't get saved. And who was this Devil, this Satan dude that seemed to be able to block everyone's good? Any time something didn't go as planned it was because the Devil was blocking the way... always, that mighty, powerful Devil.

And another thing, why were we singing about Jesus one minute and talking behind people's back the next? So what if a person wanted to smoke, miss church sometimes, or didn't want to go out and bring in souls for Jesus? Wasn't gossiping just as bad as any of the things they were wagging about? There were so many inconsistencies and questions. These things, and so many others, just didn't sit right with me.

But that didn't stop God from sending me messages loudly and clearly. I got the "calling." I would be working for the Lord. That message was as profound as anything I had ever known. The only context I could put it in during those vulnerable teenage years was to become a preacher. I felt the need to lead the congregation and the youth groups, and actually was given that opportunity, speaking to each on several occasions. I was completely dedicated to that calling. However, I left the church after a few years totally disillusioned with judgmental people, some of the rules the church said I had to live by, and that nasty ole boy, The Devil, whom I later came to realize isn't even real!

However, I still felt compelled, even driven to follow my calling. It guided me through the rest of my teens, even to the point of the college I chose. It was not a Bible college, or a religious college, but they definitely encouraged the study of the Bible. I felt I was appeasing God by keeping my promise to follow that calling.

For many years after, that still small voice inside me would occasionally stir and I would hear the whisper reminding me, "Linda, you made a promise to God." I would usually respond, "Yes, and I intend to keep that promise as soon as She/He lets me know when and what I am to do."

While I waited, I lived without a connection to a church or religion, and like so many of us do, became preoccupied with life. Although I still felt that connection to God, I kept my beliefs to myself. It would be a long time before I began to see a purpose for me, and even then it was a slow process.

The first seminar I ever gave was profound in that I felt I had come full circle. I spent all day talking about the Angels. I had kept my promise. But more importantly, I had finally heard what God had been telling me to do. I had finally figured out my true calling.

Transformation

The process of transformation for me has always been gradual; usually the angels don't fill me in on what's happening until it's on top of me. I have had many wonderful teachers along the way. Dr. Doreen Virtue has done so much to help clarify things for me. I highly recommend reading her book, *Earth Angels*. In it she describes different groups of Light Workers. There are incarnated Angels, incarnated Fairies, Star People, Walk-ins, and Wise Ones. Each group carries with it characteristics that are specific to its group. Dr. Virtue feels that each of us originate from one of those groups. And by understanding from where we originate, we get a greater understanding of ourselves and our mission. At the time I read *Earth Angels* I did not know that I would soon learn of my own origins first-hand.

One autumn day, after I had come from attending one of Dr. Virtue's seminars in Phoenix, and having read so many of her books, I was curious about learning more and was surfing her website. I scanned the list of classes and seminars and noticed one scheduled that coming February. It was an ATP course in San Diego. I had no idea what an ATP course was, but a week away in San Diego escaping the mountain winter, studying spiritual things sounded great to me! I signed up. On the first day of the course I realized it could change my life if I wanted it to, but it would not be without a very personal commitment and profound effect on my life's direction. I could get certified to do angel readings, but it would mean that I would have to claim my psychic abilities.

In my practice, as I worked with people, I would often get information, see deceased loved ones, or even help connect displaced spirits with the Light. But when asked if I was psychic I would answer, "No." I did not think that the little bit of information I "saw" once in a while qualified me as psychic. So I denied that ability, keeping it from developing. But this workshop put it in front of my face, as God and the angels do so often. During the ATP course is when I learned that Archangel Michael is one of my guides. He made it quite clear what was expected of me. I "knew" that I would be doing readings for people. But I had to make the commitment that would reveal my true spiritual nature to the world.

As the amazing week in San Diego progressed I learned more about myself, my origin, my gifts, and my beliefs. The day we discussed *Earth Angels*, Doreen explained each origin group, then asked us to leave the classroom to get together with others in our specific Earth Angel category. As everyone filed out of the room, I just stood there, not having been "assigned" to any group. A fellow classmate looked my way and walked past me saying, "Come on. We old witches are in the Wise Ones group." Not knowing what to do, I followed.

The Wise Ones are those souls who had been sorcerers or sorceresses in past lives. They had, in many lifetimes, been tortured and burned at the stake for what they believed. During the centuries when the matriarchal society was being replaced by the patriarchal society (meaning, when the Church run by men as priests, cardinals, and popes, was trying to eliminate the pagan religions, run by women as witches, priestesses, and goddesses), torture and horrendous methods of death were common ways to deal with people who refused to change.

Many innocent people, whether pagan or not, died in this way, all for the purpose of control under the guise of religion.

I accepted a place in that group because it didn't seem too far-fetched to me. Strange as it may sound, I had memories of being burned at the stake. Besides, what did it matter to me to go along with them to see what I could learn? Still, I didn't feel quite comfortable and I was more than a little skeptical. Then when we all joined hands to pray, I was convinced in a most powerful way. I had a vision. This had never before happened to me and I can't tell you how amazingly weird it was. I had just come for a vacation and here I was having, of all things, a vision! In this vision I was totally transported to another time. I was on a battlefield. There were horses, knights, and fighting going on all around me. It was as if it were happening in real time. I was there! I got the definite impression that somehow, the battle was about me. Then a knight came charging toward me with a huge sword and stabbed me in the gut! I didn't feel any pain (thank you, God!), but my body was rocked in a great spasm. I felt like I was thrust backward. And then as fast as it started, the vision was gone.

I became a believer! It was at that moment I could no longer deny my true nature, and gave in to total acceptance. I knew who I was, where I came from, and why I am here. An amazing feeling overtook me. For the first time in my life I felt totally free. I wasn't trying to pretend anymore. I claimed my God-given power. The beauty of believing in and accepting your possibilities is that you can open up to the power of your true nature. There is no more denying, no more false humility, and things get a whole lot easier. You are not doing battle with yourself anymore and you can really hear what Spirit is trying to tell you.

My studies also revealed to me what exactly was in my past lives that made the greatest impact on my current life. I have always had powerful psychic abilities. I lived lives that were full, helping to heal others. But in many lives, including this one, I hid that knowledge, my talents and gifts, even from myself. There is nothing like being burned at the stake to make you think twice about declaring who you are!

In contrast, my time between lifetimes is spent living in opulence. Gold is my power metal and I manifest what I need when I need it. When I decided to come to this life, I devised a program for myself with no opulence, no gold, where I would always settle for less than what I really wanted, and where I would feel very uncomfortable with the "me" I created for this incarnation. This helps explain my great need to be abundant, which is necessary if a body wants to be draped in gold jewelry, which I love and in which I definitely wish to be draped.

So there I was on the other side, living in opulence, my soul bathed in God's light, and having quite a good time of it, when the call went out in Heaven:

Light Workers Needed.
All Special Talents Appreciated.
Big things are happening on planet Earth!
Pick your time and the Angels will send you back.

How could I refuse? So I planned this life. I got my team together (souls I have been with before who wanted to have another go at life in my company), and this time I decided to make it especially difficult for myself. I decided there should be some heavy family dysfunction, a manic depressive and physically abusive mother, a dad who would be emotionally disconnected and who liked to crawl into bed with little girls. Then I thought wouldn't it be great if the family would have major money issues? That could set the stage for even more hard work to overcome in my adulthood! And, of course, no one would have a clue how a real family should operate. Then to top it off, I wouldn't want to, but I would forget that I am a healer and psychic and would have to learn that all over again from the ground up.

When we are on the other side in all that light and love, it's hard to remember how incredibly difficult physical life can be. For one, there is our ego to overcome. And then, none of us come with a set of instructions when we are born, at least none we are aware of. But in God's light we only see the good this plan will create, and how these opportunities will set us up for more enlightenment. In spite of, or because of the planning, we also forget that free will is always available, with a variety of paths to choose from. So options and opportunities are always there. We can take them or not.

"Believing" truly began for me during my stay in San Diego. But my journey had just begun. The angels had much in store for me, and mine was a mission of discovery before I would be given the opportunity to exercise my true calling.

First Key: Believe

Have you ever wondered why when we are born, when we come to this planet, that we don't get a little tag on our toe or a little label attached to our side that says, "Here Are Your Instructions For Life?" I mean, even the least expensive hand-held electronic game comes with an instruction booklet, usually bigger than the game itself! Are we not just as important as a battery operated Pac Man?

Well, life doesn't come with an owner's manual and we don't really get a lot of practical instruction. It seems as if we are just kind of plopped here. People have asked me, "Why doesn't God give us something to follow? Why don't we get more direct information?" We have so many questions that seem to go unanswered for most of our lives and we tend to get those answers primarily through trial and error. It's been a hard way to learn for most of us. And still we are not really sure we have done it right!

The world we were born into relies upon wonderful and ancient religious and intellectual sources such as the Bible, the Torah, the Koran, and many others, to give us the guidance we seek. But we find that, too often, we are taught or encouraged to take that guidance far too literally. To many of us that literal interpretation doesn't seem very relevant to our lives today. And we don't see how these sources can help us with questions like:

- "What can I do, right now, about this person who hates me and makes my life hell?"

- "How am I going to deal with the bills this month?"

- "How can I handle this terrible trauma in my life?"

We don't really have a "John 13:12" per se, that says we're going to get the money we need from Uncle George, or "In order to forgive and forget, do the following," or where exactly we will find within ourselves that perfect comeback to answer a put-down by that jerk that makes us crazy. We don't get something that gives us a direct message, something placed in front of us that says "Here you go. Here's your answer!"

We don't get our instructions that way. However, we are born with everything we need to receive and interpret direct guidance. We are born with incredible gifts of discernment and intuition that are intended to keep us connected to the very source of that guidance. Our gifts result in a wonderful psychic ability, which is how we were meant to communicate with the other side, the angels, Jesus, Muhammad, all of our spiritual masters, up to and including the Divine Energy itself, which I call God. In fact, each of us is at our psychic best when we are born. Babies, children, young ones, are the closest of us to God. We come to this planet already intuitively aware of the Divine Energy. We don't have to do anything to jump-start this ability or earn it. We just show up with it.

However, as we grow up we are taught that psychic communication isn't real, and that our intuition is not to be taken seriously. We are taught that unless we see it, it's not legit. We learned this from everyone, our parents, our church and school teachers, the media, and our mentors. We in turn, have passed this along to our kids, through our best intentions of course, along with other well-meaning fallacies and fables. Too many of us were first introduced to the notion of psychic connections through an entertainment source, like parlor games (Ouija Board, séances, etc.), or TV and movies, making us fearful and/or skeptical. Even the word "psychic" offends many people. If it offends you, feel free to use whatever word you want instead. But that is your means of communication with the other side, and it has been severed because we learned to ignore it. We lost our ability to hear that still, small voice that comes from our heart center that says, "Here's the direction you're supposed to go." As a result, we now miss out on that guidance and allow fear and apprehension to become major motivators in our lives.

Our intuitive gifts are lost, not only because they are not supported and encouraged, but also because we become distracted by our daily lives. We go to school, get involved in our culture, and we grow up and get caught in the way of the physical world, then find ourselves in a very demanding society. Those of you who are older, could you possibly believe that in this modern world, we could have the kind of demands on us that we have? Who among you could have imagined the immediate alarms sounded by the communications of international issues from all corners of the world, or the constant demand of your attention by email, fax machines, and cell phones... all of the modern conveniences designed to keep you in touch that too often keep you tied up?

Yes, there are big benefits to these innovations. One of the biggest is cell phones. I mean, what did parents do before kids had cell phones? I call my daughter and ask, "What are you doing, who are you with, and when are you coming home?" That I love! And because many of the phones today have a GPS system, you know where your kids are sometimes before they do! I remember once when I was a teen, I was on a date with a guy who actually got a flat tire and there was no way to contact my mother. And my mother...well, let's just say, you were never late! That just couldn't happen today. Even pay phones are hard to find anymore because everyone has a cell phone! You can call anyone anywhere at any time. Incredible! We have all these modern conveniences, these advances, but what came with these advancements are busier lives and more things that we need to pay attention to in the physical world. The physicality of the world has pushed out the spiritual part of our lives.

There are a great many of us who miss that spirituality and want to know how we get back there. How can we get the ability to know what's going on? We can read the Bible, the Tanakh, the Vedas, or the Qur'an, take classes, even meditate. But even with doing all these things, somehow we are still missing our direction, our instructions; the relevant answers to our life's questions. I think that what many of us would really like is to step outside our houses and see a great big billboard where the angels have written, "So, okay! Here's what's going to happen today and here's how you need to respond." Well, I haven't seen that billboard yet. I don't think that's coming around any time soon. You might be able to manifest one if you try hard enough, but it might take a great deal of effort. Really, finding the guidance you need is a lot easier than that.

So as we grow up we are actually taught not to use the natural way of communicating with God. The irony is that God sets us up with everything we need to get along in this world. But we are taught exactly the opposite. We are taught that God is in Heaven. We are taught that we are sinners and are separated from God. We are taught that God only talks directly to "pure" people, or "righteous" people, or "chosen" people. And we are sure that we are none of those. We are taught that we need to suffer, that it's okay to be sick, that we need to sacrifice, that poverty is a good way to be spiritual. We are taught that worry and stress and guilt are sure ways to get you a place in Heaven because engaging in these shows that you care, and good people care, and good people go to Heaven. We are taught so many things, most of which demonstrate the need to be afraid. Fear is taught early and reinforced throughout our lives.

How does this lead up to "The Eight Keys to the Kingdom," and specifically to the Key of Belief? Most people I meet just can't believe what I do. They look at me like I have three heads and a tail. "What do you do?" they ask, incredulously. "Do you actually think you communicate with angels?" Well, yes, I do! Everybody can. It's not something to be amazed by. Everybody is born with that gift. You have that gift too and you can use that gift. The problem is that I believe it and most of you don't. I know it and you have doubt. That's the only difference. When you believe that you can do it too, that's when you can get back the tool God intended to use to communicate with you. Fear is a huge hurdle between you and that belief. So how do you get beyond that? Well first...

During my seminar at the expo the day before the first presentation of what I have come to call "The Keys," I was inviting my audience to come hear about the "Eight Keys to the Kingdom" when someone asked me, "Which kingdom?" That's a really good question. We all know that Heaven is a great place, but which Heaven is the one we want to get to? And whose Heaven are we talking about? Think of all the varied religions of the world, some based on ancient teachings, some on newer trains of thought and every variation on a theme. We've got people willing to take their airplanes and run them into buildings, or strap bombs to their bodies to take out a bus or a plaza full of people because they believe that when they get to the other side they are supposed to meet up with great rewards for their sacrifice. We all know people who have, or who want to check out of this world, because their circumstances are just too challenging and they don't want to struggle with those challenges any more. There are people who would rather keep their eye on the next world because this one is just not meeting their needs. Those who live for death or life on the other side, miss the whole point of being here. They just want to skip the whole earthly planet thing and head over to the other side, because they believe it's going to be better there.

Yes, it can be better there. But if we miss the point in this life we just have to come back and do it again. So let's just get it now! Let's do it right this time around.

This book is about the Kingdom of Heaven, but these Eight Keys are about creating the Kingdom of Heaven here on Earth. It is about bringing the Kingdom of Heaven into your life, into your daily communications, into your day by day interactions. It's about bringing the Kingdom of Heaven into you. And the only way – that's why this particular topic is first – the only way you're going to get the Kingdom of Heaven into your physical life is if you BELIEVE you can have it.

So, what is the Kingdom, basically? Well, what attracts us to Heaven? Some of us speak of Heaven as "home," where we can expect to find comfort and release from worldly cares. We also expect it to be a place where there is love, peace, abundance, joy, happiness, and being one with the Divine. Can we really have this on Earth? Yes, by believing. To believe is to change your life. You need to believe in something besides just what you see in front of you. When people tell us stories about finding belief and how it changed their lives, those are not mere stories at all. They are truths! They are miracles!

Everything we have been taught says that it can't possibly happen, we can't have Heaven on Earth, miracles don't happen in our modern times, and if it did they would only happen to someone else. We have been taught that we can't know what the future holds for us, our circumstances are determined by "destiny" and that can't be changed. Everything around us says that in the real world you get what you deserve, you have to be afraid, you have to get out there and work your butt off in order to just get a smidgen of the good that is out there to get, and it's wrong to want a larger share. You need to know that all of this is not true.

The fact that I ended up with a beautiful baby girl a day after she was born is a miracle. (You can read that story at the end of this chapter). Miracles didn't just happen in olden times. They happen every day, right now. Do you think that miracles happen just to other people? They don't have to! In order to have miracles in your life you first have to believe that you can. In believing, you go beyond what you can see. You move beyond what is directly in front of you, from the physical realm into the spiritual. To believe, you must be willing to go beyond what you were taught and that may be the biggest thing you will ever do in your life!

So what is it again about Heaven that's so great? Being a medium, I have many times talked to those on the other side and they tell me it's a very nice place. They talk of how, when they let go of their physical body, the stress went away. So we know there is no stress in Heaven. They tell me how peaceful it is. So we know that everything there is in harmony. And they tell me they don't have to worry anymore. So we know Heaven has no problems, physical, emotional, or spiritual. Can we have some of that on Earth? Can we actually let go of the stress? Can we just be peaceful, enjoy one another, live in harmony? Can we have what we need when we need it? Can our physical bodies be pain free, stronger, and well? Can we have less chaos, less fear, less anger? Can we actually have the Kingdom of Heaven here on Earth, in our lives, at this moment?

Yes, if you believe.

And there are some that don't, and some who won't, and some who can't. And maybe even now, you are saying, "Oh, that is absolutely crazy…there is no possible way. You don't have any idea of the situations that I have to deal with, or the relatives I have to put up with, or the difficulties I have at my job. You just don't have a clue!"

And you are right. I don't. I don't have a clue what you're going through. Nor do I care!

That may seem callous of me to say that I don't care. I probably seem downright cold and heartless. But I know you can make up all kinds of excuses that allow you to stay in those difficult situations. You can convince yourself that you can't change a thing, that believing has never made a difference in your world. But I say, you have just believed you could not change. You have believed you don't deserve better. You have believed you can't make a difference. You can continue to believe this or you can choose to believe you can have this Kingdom. It is a choice. And the choice is yours. And that I do care about.

The angels are handing you the first key. And they are saying, "Believe it!" What they're presenting to you is going beyond what you know to be real in your life. They want you to take a step out of the norm, out of your own personal comfort zone and say, "I'm willing to open up to something different, something more; something beyond this physical world." And they're going to bring Heaven right into your living room.

So what is it we are to believe? Let's just say, hypothetically, that every single one of us decides right now to try this whole "belief thing." What we believe is that a power greater than we is out there. We believe that this power is "Love Energy" and that power can transmute anything negative in our lives and bring us Heaven on Earth. Believe that that power can change anything negative in your life!

Let's go as far as to believe that this Love Energy can take care of that nasty boss, your financial worries, physical illness, or any issue, situation or limitation you may have. Now the angels are aware that we, as 3-D human beings, can't totally comprehend that a power outside of ourselves can actually affect our daily lives, and the people in it, simply because we believe that it can. This will be hard for some of us to accept. It doesn't make logical sense to us. Listen! This doesn't have anything to do with our logic.

The angels now ask you to take an even bigger step into "I Believe," to the realm of four dimensions. In that dimension, the dimension of Belief, the logic works. We can imagine that it's getting even tougher for some people to grasp now. But I'm telling you the effort is worth it. When you go to four dimensions they (the angels, God, and our spiritual guides and teachers) start downloading. They start giving you information and making changes. You start driving to work one day and they tell you, "You know, you're going to have a little bit of trouble today. All you have to do is send love into the situation."

But you have to do your part. You need to believe and the information will come to you. Is it that easy? Yes. Does this make sense? No! But it will. That is the logic. You believe and then you begin to receive the instructions for life you wanted from the beginning. Yes, you get access to the manual! I know you think it's weird. It's even weird for me. I am constantly surprised at how the logic works. I had to believe that in just stepping up to the church podium to deliver this message the angels would tell me what they wanted you to know. And they did. I had no outline in my head. I didn't have any notes. But I believed. I started talking and the information flowed.

Now that we have taken ourselves to the fourth dimension, let's go farther. Let's say that everything that's in your life, everything that has happened before, everything now that is happening, and everything that will happen tomorrow is Divine.

Believe it. Now get into the habit of saying, "It's all good. It's... all... good!"

Tell yourself, "I may not understand it. I don't know why this chaos is here. But the angels say that we're supposed to believe. So here's this chaotic situation...here's money I owe...here's this person who's attacking me...here's this boss whom I just can't stand...but I believe there's a power bigger than me. So I'm going to invite the angels in and tell them, "Okay, angels, (or God, or Jesus, or Divine Energy), take care of this. I don't want this person to be in my life. I don't want this situation to be in my life. I don't know where the money is coming from for this thing. Take care of it, please. And I'm going to believe."

For that minute, for just one minute, you decide to let go. Your shoulders relax, and all of a sudden you're not stressing. It lasts for about sixty seconds and it's a great feeling.

But you know how you are. "Yeah, okay. Here comes the boss now. Okay, this bill is still lying on the table..." But for that sixty seconds you sent out the pure energy of belief. And I'll tell you what – there's something in that whole thing about a grain of mustard seed. Having just that small amount of faith can move a mountain! For sixty seconds you sent pure energy out that you totally believed. That energy goes out and when it comes back to you it brings exactly what you need.

But – and I can attest to this! – it never shows up in the manner in which you think it should. Never. So along with believing, let's let go of expectations of how the whole issue should be resolved. Expectations are blinders. When you have those blinders on your solution is going to come from a direction that you are not going to be able to see. I have clients come back to me after beginning this process to say, "I don't know what happened here. It's like nothing has happened. Nothing is fixed. I still have this problem." When this happens, and it will happen, talk to the angels. You missed something. Talk to God. You've missed something somewhere. Because when you believe, and you send out that energy, and you say, "Take care of this, God. Handle this, God," you will get an answer every single time. You are never ignored. Those clients that say, "God's not hearing me!" Uh-uh! Impossible. They just didn't get the answer in the way they expected it, in the way they wanted it, or they didn't get what they wanted. But the answer came. And it came with Divine Energy, which means, It's all good. "It's... all... good!"

I spent what seemed like eternity before we got our daughter – somewhere around four years – going through infertility tests, surgeries, drugs, all kinds of different methods and treatments trying to get pregnant. And every single night I prayed that God would send me the answer. And when it came it shocked me. Not that I got the answer, but that it came in a manner that I had nothing to do with. Nothing I did brought that baby to me. I was pushing and shoving for all those years and nothing I was trying to accomplish happened. The baby came to us, and I had nothing to do with it.

Now, can you imagine how hard it was for an incredibly controlling person like me to understand that I had nothing to do with that baby coming to us? I could take no credit whatsoever. I had to totally let go of my expectations, and to let go of control! As I looked at that little tiny baby in the bassinette, I thought, "Wow, I guess God really does know what She's doing." Because in the end when it all came together, it was the simplest, easiest, most joyful experience I could've possibly had. And it had nothing at all to do with my efforts. But somewhere in those moments of prayer, in those moments of begging, in those moments of despair, there was sixty seconds of total belief that I knew God was going to answer, and I knew that it was taken care of.

I give you this: If you can just put out sixty seconds of belief, one little minute, you can put out two minutes. And you can increase that belief to an hour. And then pretty soon your life is going to be 24/7 of "It's all good. God's going to take care of it. I don't have to worry about anything. I believe. I believe."

But you need to practice. Not believing and not having faith is a habit. Worry is a habit. Stressing over big things or little things like money is a habit. I say money is a "little thing" because I want you to grasp the concept that money is a little thing. It is just energy. The less importance you give it, the more it will flow to you. But you've got to believe. For sixty seconds you've got to believe. This will help to break these habits of a life time. Many of us came off the tail end of the Great Depression, or had parents or grandparents that came out of that era, and we were taught to store and put away, to be afraid, and to worry about the future. Preparing for a rainy day in order to cover your options for your future is a great idea. But don't let it rule your life. You need to let go of that habit of constant worry. Because everything you need will come to you if you only believe. Sixty seconds. Just sixty seconds of pure belief is all I'm asking of you right now.

I would like you to know that I've been practicing this for a long time. I know these habits and how hard they are to overcome because I am a very stubborn, high maintenance, materialistic person. I really love "things." I know that about myself and I'm okay with that. But in order to get these "things," to have the abundance to get these "things," I had to have a lot of faith. I had to quit worrying and I had to believe. And now for me, it's just 24-7. Something shows up, anything that comes my way, and I automatically think, "Okay! It's divine. It's all good. It's...all...good."

That's the place I want you to reach. That's where I want you to go. That's what I want you to practice. When an issue comes up and you're back into the habit of "Where's the rent money coming from, what about my health, what about this and what about that?" I want you, for just sixty seconds, to send out pure belief. And in that sixty seconds, let your shoulders go, "Ahhh!" Because you just took off that big heavy backpack you carry that contains all that stress and worry that you were taught you're supposed to have. You're breaking habits of a lifetime. Have you ever tried to quit smoking? How hard is that? How about trying to give up sugar? That's even harder! So you know how hard it is to break habits. This is not any different. You are in the habit of worrying. You are in a habit of looking around for the physical stuff of "how is this going to be solved...where is the money coming from...how am I going to get what I need...how do I make this payment...where am I going to get a job...how do I make this all work?"

You hear that? How do *I* make this all work? Back up. You're on the wrong path. It has nothing to do with you. In the end, when you choose to believe, nothing you do is going to bring it around. God's going to put it all in order. She's going to create synchronicity. And let me tell you, if you're supposed to do something the angels will tell you. God will tell you. You will know. You will be compelled — "I've got to get over there!" "I have to do this!" Did you ever have that experience where you're supposed to turn right, but felt the need to turn left instead? People have turned up at my store saying, "Gosh, I just had to get in here! I just had to come. It was just like I was being pulled."

You'll be guided because that's what believing is all about. You're not going to be guided by fear. It's not going to be panic or, the best one, obsession, when you get it into your head that "I have to take care of this!" even when you have no clue of what to do. You find yourself running in ten different directions, yet can't come up with a solution. I can be obsessive-compulsive. I know how this works. Obsession, worry, fear! They are all habits.

Just start with sixty seconds of "I Believe," pure belief. And then start breaking away from those habits. Start breaking the energy of fear. Start breaking the energy of stress. All of a sudden you are stepping into the Kingdom. Do you really think that God just dumped you here with nothing? It's impossible. We are constantly connected to the ever flowing Love Energy. And everything you need and every experience you have is Divine! You just don't think it is…yet.

Just because you have the Kingdom of Heaven on Earth and in your life, and will learn about these eight keys, doesn't mean you'll never have a challenge come up in your life. I'm not going to use the word "problem," because I don't believe in problems. There are no such things. I'm going to say issues, circumstances, challenges that come into your life. You will have things that happen. You will have people that will say things that will hurt your feelings. You will have people that will come to you that might try to ruin your day. You're still going to have issues in your life.

Do you know what the difference is going to be? It won't matter. It won't matter because you believe, because you know it's all divine and because you're connected to an energy that makes you think, "Hmm, if this person (or situation) makes me feel uncomfortable, then there must be something I need to look at in my life." Take that experience and ask God how you can benefit from it. Look for and find the positive in it. Ask the Divine Creator to help you go with the flow of that situation. Every experience you have turns into an opportunity for growth, a blessing. It is a divine situation, because, it is given to you for your best and highest good! It's…all…good!

Just start this week, this day, now, with sixty seconds, sixty small seconds of total belief that you're going to send out there to the universe, to the angels, to God.

The whole universe supports what you do when you follow this path. There is nothing of lack on your path at all! If you are seeing lack you are looking in the wrong direction, because there is no such thing. The universe will not allow there to be a void, a hole, a lack in your life. God will fill it with whatever it is you need…as long as you believe it's all good, it's all divine.

Now that you have begun this journey of change by believing, you can begin to "expect." You can expect that when you take a journey like this, the angels are going to put in front of your face exactly what you need to deal with. And some of that is not very pleasant. So expect it. And when it shows up, just say, "Okay, God. I'm going to remember what the angels said and I'm just going to believe."

With that Key of Belief in your hand you can now ask, "What is the divine in this situation?" I have experience with some of those unpleasant moments myself. I asked the angels to help me expand my business and they brought an opportunity to me to purchase some very expensive equipment for treating health issues, to strengthen the energy around the body. The expense made me very nervous. But I took the chance anyway. With the installation of the equipment business got better. But when I realized just how much money I was starting to make I suddenly felt incredibly uncomfortable and almost guilty. I hadn't expected to feel that way and certainly didn't want to deal with those kinds of feelings. I felt guilt for making money, fear for asking others to support what I know works! I started in with my angels, "Wait a minute! What's this all about?!" And in that moment I realized, "Holy smoke! It's divine." It took a little time for the enlightenment to come that I'm okay with putting myself out on that financial limb. I love the little universal "Ah Haaas" that show up when I least expect it. I realized that with the abundance I'm getting I am able to give more to others in need, and to the church that I love. And very importantly, I can put more into my business to bring good health and enlightenment to more people.

But even more than that, this kind of success is what I asked for! It is what I prayed for! The freedom to come and go, the freedom to be financially abundant! And I'm getting it because I believe. Be careful for what you ask, because you're going to get it! Pay attention to those feelings and issues as they happen to you and release the negativity as it comes up, because the angels are going to give you everything that you need. All you have to do is believe.

You have just read about the first Key to the Kingdom, "Believe." Some of you may not read all of the next seven Keys. You may only get through three or four or this may be the only one you read. I'm okay with that, because I know you will get out of this book what you need, regardless of whether you read one page or the whole thing. However far you read, whatever information you get, is going to change your life if you allow it. It will change what comes to you, what happens to you. And it will all be good, because it is all divine.

It may not always be comfortable and it may not always show up in the manner that you expect. But it's always divine.

If you get nothing else from this book, just put on your tongue, "I believe!"

Meditation #1

Take time to meditate. Relax.

Visualize yourself taking off the big heavy backpack that contains all your worries, all your angers, all your fears. Just take it off and let your shoulders drop. Relax. Imagine God is there to take the big heavy backpack from you. I always see Jesus standing in front of me saying, "I'll take that! I can handle it. Give me that backpack."

Picture in your head the image of the Love Energy you want to give your backpack to. Now believe that Entity will handle it.

Believe that you never have to pick up that backpack again because it belongs to God now.

Take your first sixty seconds of pure belief. For sixty seconds everything you need is coming to you. It's all divine, and it's all good. Everyone in your life is a blessing. Everything that's happening in your life is there because it's divine. And you have total belief that this life here on Earth is all good.

Close your eyes for sixty seconds and know that it's all good. "It's...all...good."

You just sent out sixty seconds of pure belief! You send it out and your good comes back to you. Expect it.

And just keep doing it in sixty second increments. Whether you're driving or at the stop light, wherever you can work it in, just know that "It's...all...good."

And keep telling yourself "I believe!"

Linda's Story: Oh, Baby!

Believing in something bigger than me, in God, in Jesus, came easy for me, starting when I was a young teenager. But it was not until I was grown that believing became real to me. "Believing" became a living, breathing presence in my daily life.

After years of searching for ways to remove myself from negativity, I found I was in the first stable relationship of my life. My husband, Scott, had been patient with me while my psyche came to believe in that stability. He had continued to love me until I finally understood that love did not always have to hurt, nor did love always leave. He was in my life to stay and that was very okay with me! Life had become peaceful and smooth, and we felt that our relationship was strong enough that it was time to have a baby.

As is my custom with any new objective, I threw myself into achieving this one with all my energy, thoughts, and gusto. I just knew I would have no problem getting pregnant. I expected that we should have a baby within the year. When the first few months had no positive results, I was surprised. I did the research, charted my cycles, took my temperature, increased some vitamins, and had sex on cue.

Month after month…no baby. My life began to run in thirty-day cycles of disappointment followed by new hope. In the beginning I was anxious to share my feelings with friends and receive their eager inquires and advice. But after a while I stopped talking about it. It was just too depressing. After the first two years of this emotional roller coaster, trying everything with the help of modern science and a local doctor, my spirit was taking a beating. Medicine could find neither reasons nor results. So I began looking into adoption. There was no adoption agency in our area of the state. So I put together letters of our intent to adopt and sent them out to various doctor's offices around the state. I then made an appointment with a family attorney and gave him a retainer in case we found a baby to adopt.

For the following two years we continued our desperate attempts to conceive, even enlisting the help of specialists of in-vitro fertilization in Phoenix. Despite successful harvesting of many of my eggs through several surgeries, none of the eggs resulted in a pregnancy. Science can be so wonderful when it works. When it doesn't, not only can it be physically painful, but it can also be devastatingly disappointing and degrading.

Throughout my life my victories had been hard won. But I won, nonetheless. I was always able to make things happen eventually. I figured if I worked hard enough, pushed hard enough, I could overcome the odds. But now, wanting a baby and not getting one, trying to work all the angles, pushing the limits on what could be done medically and trying to find someone who could get me a baby to adopt, nothing was working for me. I had tried everything from herbs to fertility drugs to surgery; made schedules and lived by them, had tests done on both Scott and me, spent so much money and suffered so much agony. What was left to do? Nothing! I had done it all.

The tremendous disappointment is not describable. I could not believe it, but it was true: I would never give birth to a child. I had heard nothing about a baby to adopt from any of the doctors I had been contacting over the years. I wasn't sure what I was going to do, since my hope had been erased. I had made all those plans for all those years. Then suddenly, there was just nothing. An emotional quietness, eerie and lonely, settled in on me. I did something in that instant I had never done before: I quit. I gave up. I threw in the towel. No more fighting. No more pushing. "Just let it go away, God. Take away the pain. I have nothing left to give. I can't do this anymore."

But as I had been making all those plans, God was putting together another. You know the saying, "If you want to make God laugh show Her your plan!" Shortly after the news of the last negative pregnancy test, a "last ditch" attempt, a friend called to check on me. Although for years I had not talked about my conception failures or at all about adoption, I had shared with this friend our hopes for this one last attempt. His reaction to the news will be etched on my memory for the rest of my life. He said, "You know, I was just in Idaho to visit my sister and her daughter is seventeen and pregnant. They've decided to give the baby up for adoption. I would have told you about it, but I didn't think you wanted to adopt. Do you think you might consider it now?"

I was in shock! You hear stories of the incredible miracles of people being in the right place at the right time, but I never thought it would ever happen for me. I had to fight tooth and nail for everything that came my way! I told him to get on the phone right that moment and call his sister and tell her I was interested. The sister, Patty, agreed to speak to me the next day.

There were things Patty and her husband wanted us to agree to, one being to keep them informed of the baby's progress. All of their requests seemed reasonable. Although at that point anything seemed reasonable to me, and there is probably not much I wouldn't have agreed to. Patty said they would call back the next day after discussing the details with their daughter.

Waiting twenty-four hours for her answer seemed like a lifetime. I prepared myself for the daughter to say no, because it was a real possibility. Her parents were giving her that choice. About the middle of the next day I got a funny feeling in the pit of my stomach. It was going to happen! Holy smokes, could this really be it?

The phone was ringing when I got home from work a little after 5 P.M. It was Patty. "Well, it looks like you and Scott are going to be parents."

I was dumbfounded. We made some arrangements and I hung up the phone. Scott pulled up into the driveway a few minutes later, and as he got out of the car, I shouted from the house, "We are going to get this baby!" The look on his face was priceless.

I moved with my usual swift and efficient speed. I needed to contact our attorney, but it had been two years since the only time I had met with him. When I called I was told he was now a judge! Oh, great! Now what do I do? His office told me to call the attorney that took over his practice and tell him my story. I called right away, again not expecting much. However, when I told the new attorney who I was, he said – and I'm not making this up – "I was just going over the files for the practice and I have yours right here in front of me." I told him we had found a baby and he said he would take care of everything.

I couldn't believe that things were finally working out for me! I was in total shock! There is one other piece of information I need to share with you to help you understand how completely amazing this whole thing was turning out to be. When Patty called to say we were getting this baby – a wonder in itself – what was even more astonishing was the baby was due in just three weeks! When working within Divine Energy amazing things happen. Synchronicity is all around. The path is paved with gold, things fall into place with amazing speed and efficiency. There is almost no effort on our part. The trouble is, most of the time we don't know this. So instead of enjoying the Divine Energy we continue to worry. And yes, worry I did as I waited the longest three weeks of my life.

Three weeks later, on Thursday, I was driving home from work and I had a "feeling" that our baby's mother was going into labor. The deal was I would get a call when she went into labor so Scott and I could be there when our baby was born. But there was no call. The next morning there was no call. I thought I must be wrong. I had not yet begun to explore my psychic abilities and was not very confident in my intuition.

On Friday afternoon I got a call from Patty, "You have a beautiful baby girl."

"WOW! When did your daughter go into labor?" I asked.

"Last night a little after 5 P.M.," Patty answered. There was so much, "Wow!" going off in my head that I almost did not hear her tell me that they didn't call because they wanted to spend that time with the baby, it being their only time alone with her. What she said didn't register, so the little alarm bells in my head did not go off. Within a few hours, Scott and I were on our way to Idaho, custody papers in hand. We drove into Patty's driveway Saturday night. Patty came out to meet us in the driveway. She told us her daughter had changed her mind.

Of course, I knew that could happen. But I just wouldn't let myself think that it would. "You've come so far," she said, as my heart pounded and the rush of blood to my head made me dizzy. "Come inside and see her."

What else could we do? We went in. As I stepped inside, I saw their daughter holding her baby. They looked exactly alike. I melted. I knew then there was no way I could take this baby from her mother. No possible way. Their whole family was there, including the great-grand parents, offering their loving support to this young girl in whatever decision she made. We tried to talk a few minutes, but Scott and I just sat there frozen with emotion.

Then the most amazing thing happened. That seventeen-year old new mother got up, walked over to me and placed baby, Jessica, in my arms. She said, crying, "I know now I'm doing the right thing." She was crying, I was crying, everyone was crying. I was still in shock wondering if I was doing the right thing taking a baby from its mother. The girl left quickly and her family was overwhelmed that she did this wise, unselfish thing. I was too.

After we got home with our precious little bundle, I remember sitting on the edge of the bed looking at my beautiful little baby girl. Looking into her deep, dark eyes, holding her preciously small and perfect hand, I had an "Ah-ha" moment. It struck me that nothing I did brought this beautiful child into my life. All of my effort, all of the torture I put myself through, all of the stress, had nothing to do with bringing this miracle to me.

I knew in that moment I had no control over anything. This wonderful life-changing event occurred not because of me, but in spite of me. While I was trying to move heaven and earth to get a baby, God was behind the scenes taking care of all the details, weaving this beautiful tapestry into my life. First, I apologized to God for all the nasty things I had said to Him – He actually did hear my prayers. And then, I thanked Him.

I have learned since that time that things go so much easier when I just get out of the way and let God and the angels do it. After all, that's what they do best. But at that time, in that "Ah-ha" moment, I was just beginning to learn that God was in control and not I.

Second Key: Trust

I stood looking out over the bright and eager faces of the congregation of the Unity Church of the White Mountains. It was nearly time to begin the presentation of the second Key to the Kingdom. Once again, I didn't have a clue what I was going to talk about, just the name of the Key. The angels instructed me to just get up there in front of everyone and they would guide me. I was not to worry. Everything would be fine. I was standing in front of about one-hundred people with no idea what I was to say, and I was not supposed to get anxious? Right!

As I was quickly trying to do an outline in my head anyway, it struck me that although the church was nearly filled, the front row was empty. I wondered if they were intimidated by me. Certainly not, I thought. I had known most of those people for many years! I laughed to myself wondering if it was, like the old joke, because I spit when I talk! Once again, the angels took my mind off of my anxiety, this time with funny little nonsensical thoughts. And of course, distracted me again from formatting an outline! As usual, everything turned out just fine. Even after so many years of working with the angels, from time to time, I still have to be reminded that they always keep their promises. I just have to relax and trust.

"Trust" is the subject of the second Key. But before we get into that Key, let me expand a little on the first Key. At the first presentation I had asked everyone to pray for Jessie, who was very homesick while traveling in Germany. I, and all the good people in that church that morning, had sent angels and thoughts of love, strength, and wellness, and we took for granted that they would reach Jessie and take care of her. We believed they would. We trusted that they would. And they did.

In the last chapter we discussed "believing." We have to believe that there actually can be a Kingdom of Heaven on Earth. "Believing" leads to "Trust." To practice believing we geared ourselves toward sixty seconds of total belief. In that sixty seconds we worked at letting go of doubts and fears, and chose to believe that we could actually have the Kingdom of Heaven on Earth.

I encourage you to continue daily meditations to increase that sixty seconds to twenty-four/seven. But I want you to understand that in the first sixty seconds, that first moment you allowed yourself to totally believe, everything shifted. That first moment put the universe in motion for you. And every additional moment of believing reinforces that first one.

I have a wonderful computer program that I work with using Frequency Medicine. In one particular part of the program, when the client has reached the goal of 100% of the frequency, the computer plays Mendelssohn's Hallelujah Chorus jubilantly, singing "Hallelujah" in celebration. Every time I hear this celebration I think about "believing." When one person takes that first sixty seconds, the angels on the other side sing, "Hallelujah," and they start shifting things. Everything starts to change because you've given them an opening to create a new path.

Before you started believing that there could be a Kingdom of Heaven on Earth, you were on a path that was filled with all the "normal" heavy energy that we have become accustomed to: worry, fear, anxiety, anger, frustration, etc. When you chose to take that first sixty seconds, you opened up possibilities. The angels jumped on that opportunity to help you, cheered, "Hallelujah," and began scurrying around behind the scenes creating another path for you.

As I began to think about how I would deliver this Key, "Trust," it occurred to me that the angels had not included "faith" in the original list. So I told them that I didn't understand and asked them why faith was not included as a Key. I thought perhaps it was because faith is the same thing as trust. I was wrong.

The angels explained that "Faith" is something you have after you believe, and after you have gone through the work of "Trust." Faith is a noun. Faith is something you acquire; it belongs to you after you trust. Trust is a verb. It's the act of trusting; you're moving toward faith. "Faith is the substance of things hoped for, the evidence of things not seen." (Hebrews 11:1, King James version.)

The last chapter may have left you enthused. "Yeah, I believe! Sixty seconds, and my whole life is changing. Things are shifting, my new road is open!"

But you look around and are still faced with the same issues, the same bills, and the same people to deal with. You still have the same job and everything you see continues, it seems, in the same manner. So you go back and grab another sixty seconds of belief, and another and then another. But the believing begins to get a little thin. It's kind of hard to grasp that things are changing because you don't see a lot going on. So you begin to question if the angels are really making that new path for you. That's when you need to remember to make your next move, to trust.

Now, the work begins. Trusting is a little more difficult than believing. This is where you must put that verb, "trust," to work. A whole lot is going on, but much of it is going on behind the scenes. That new path is being created based on your true heart's desire. "But," you say, "I don't see that new path. Nothin's happen'n here." When you still see that pile of bills, or still have those people to deal with, or you go to work and there are still those conditions in front of you, say this affirmation:

"God, I'm going to trust you."

That kicks the verb into action and begins the process of trusting. Even if you are not sure you do trust, just saying it will begin allowing trust to grow within you.

It's like becoming a runner. You don't begin on day one doing five miles around the block. Have you ever tried that? It just doesn't happen on the first go 'round. You have to build up stamina over time by running a little more each day. It's the same thing with trust. Put out a little more trust each time you say the affirmation, and before you know it, you are trusting. When you put that action, that energy of trust, out there, you will find that things begin to change.

In putting all of the Eight Keys to the Kingdom together the angels also gave me affirmations. I did not create them, nor did the angels. But they know a great thing when they see it! The affirmations are by Florence Scovel-Shinn from her books, *The Secret of Success* and *The Game of Life and How to Play It*. If you haven't read her books, I highly recommend them. Florence Scovel-Shinn was an artist and metaphysics teacher in the early part of the 20th century and wrote from the 1920s until her death in 1940. Her teachings were very advanced for the time. Her books are still in print today and are available in many book stores and on the web. Some of the affirmations the angels wanted to bring forth are:

I do not resist this situation!
I'm not struggling against it.
When I put it in the hands of Infinite Love and
Wisdom, the divine idea comes to pass.

So as you face that pile of bills, that person you must deal with, the frustrations of recurring unpleasant issues, the doubt that Belief has opened a new path for you, say again, and again if you must, "I do not resist this situation! I'm not struggling against it. When I put it in the hands of Infinite Love and Wisdom, the divine idea comes to pass."

As you practice the affirmations and use them in your life; as you stop to remember that you have already given the situation to God, especially those that particularly stress you; as you remind yourself that the great Love Energy of the universe will always handle what you give it, trust begins to get stronger. Trust will grow within you to the point that each time you find yourself in doubt, or in stress, or in fear you will automatically begin saying: "I do not resist this situation. I do not resist. I am not battling against. I am not pushing forward. I am not going to hurt anyone. I am not going to run over anybody. I am not going to do anything. I do not resist. This situation has been given to me. And God, I want you to bless it! I give it to you to handle."

You will find that the more trust grows, the more control you give up. And the more you let the outcome go, the more you will grow in faith! You will not have to work at it anymore. You will simply just have faith. Because you believe, and because you trust, you have faith. You live in faith.

Now because you believe, your new path is laid out before you. Because you are exercising the verb of trust, the energy in your life begins to shift, and you cannot expect that things are going to go smoothly. I cannot emphasize this enough. You will definitely experience a few bumps. Why is that? Change, of course! You let God in and as I have seen many, many times, no energy, no person, nothing in this universe, can screw up your life the way God can. This energy of love that goes through the whole universe will come in and start shifting everything. You begin believing and praying for change, for help, for growth, for success, for whatever, and then you begin to see things happen. But they're not what you expected. People I have counseled have come back to me and said, "Well, look what happened! This is just falling apart. I can't believe this. I was praying for my grandson and look what happened to him!"

Wait a minute! Where is your trust? You opened up the door and told God to come into your life, told Her that you wanted these Keys to the Kingdom, said you didn't like the way things were going. You said you wanted love, peace, joy and abundance in your life!

And God said, "OK. Let's do it! In order for you to have the Kingdom this has got to change…and that has got to change…and everything over there has got to change."

As change starts to become evident in your life, you get very nervous, unsettled and you say, "Wait a minute! My whole life is changing. I don't have anything here that I am familiar with. This path is unknown to me. I don't know what is going on. Everything is so chaotic. Everything is different."

Well, remember, when you throw clothes in a washing machine they are going to get very agitated before they get clean. And it is no different with your life.

This is why the second Key, "Trust" is so important. If the way you were doing things was so good and worked so well, you would not be concerned with making your life better. Obviously the path before this has not worked so well. So when you take the steps and say, "Okay, God. Come into my life, make these changes for me," don't be surprised when the changes show up. The problem is that we humans really hate change! We want change, we pray for change, but we don't expect that so much has to change to just get the changes we want! That's why we have to trust.

What did you think was going to happen? You could think that God would just take away all your issues, and then drop that basket of million dollars on the front porch. That would be nice, but it doesn't work that way. That doesn't mean you're not going to get that million dollars you are praying for. It just means that some changes have to go on before a million dollars is going to show up in your life. But unless you trust, nothing's going to happen. When you trust, you will find that all of a sudden, you are in the midst of change. And some changes may be very dramatic. Maybe you will be leaving your job, or a spouse, or maybe changing where you live. Maybe the angels want you to write a book, like they asked me to do, or go back to school, or adopt a child, or open a business, or close your business, or any number of things that you never even thought of doing before. And it just scares the pants off of you!

We can continue to resist the changes, give in to that fear, or we can choose to move toward the life for which we prayed. The responsibility for making that choice is ours. We could choose to live with all the heavy, negative energy, and be like the people who don't take responsibility for their lives. We all know those people.

They would just as soon blame the government, blame their boss, or their job, or their friends, for the unhappiness, dissatisfaction, victimhood, in their lives. How about this one: "Oh, the way my parents raised me totally screwed me up." We can blame whomever we want to blame and our lives will continue to be on that low level with the heavy energies of fear, guilt, anger, doubt, depression, sadness, resentment; all of those negative emotions.

Those people who have decided to blame everything outside themselves have given away their power. You can continue to live like that, choose to be powerless too, but you don't have to. You can choose to understand that you are the one that needs to take responsibility for what goes on in your life. Once you grasp that, believe that, you are ready to be empowered. The only way that you can be empowered is to trust. Trust that there is an energy much more potent and loving than any one of us could ever be, and that power is handling your affairs – once you believe and once you trust!

When we hand over our affairs to God, we finally take them out of the hands of amateurs, and that includes ourselves. We're taking back our power and we're putting it in the hands of the Divine. We're turning over our lives to the experts. If you've ever done accounting all by yourself, or computer repair, or tried to work on your car, or your washing machine, and just made things worse and had to hand those issues over to experts, they probably had to make a lot of significant changes in order to get things working right, including undoing a lot of your "fixes." The experts came in and took over, and you were at their mercy! But you trusted them, you paid big bucks for those experts, and they came in and identified what in your lifestyle, or work style, had to change in order to avoid getting things messed up again. Basically, they shifted everything in your life. Do you think that the Almighty would do any less?

But here's the good news. It's free! The Divine Energy will totally come into your life, and change things around, and totally screw things up for free! All you have to do is trust! You put your life, your expectations, your heart's desire, into the hands of the experts – God the Mother, God the Father, God the Holy Spirit – and then things become chaotic. Everything around you starts moving very quickly. Change is coming into your life. And change, my friends, is the hardest thing we must deal with.

Practice the affirmation again each time you are feeling uneasy, unsure, or overwhelmed with the changes that begin to appear:

"I do not resist this situation. I do not resist this situation. I…do not…resist…this situation."

There are people in abusive relationships that will stay in those relationships year after year just to resist change! They stay with what they know to avoid the unknown. But the universe revolves on change. The universe is in constant flux. If you are going to put yourself in divine energy, which some would say, you've found this book in order to do, you are going to have to go with the flow and accept that change is going to be a major part of your life. Change is the natural process by which we grow, learn, progress, and benefit. With change you come to know that which you have not known before. And just when you get comfortable, just when you get peaceful, just when you think, "Aha, I've got it," guess what? Here comes some more change! And you are going to realize, "Here's another thing I'm supposed to 'get.'"

How many times can we get those universal "Ahas," where the elevator goes all the way to the top, and the lights are all on in the attic? How many times can that happen in your life? It's too infinite to count. So expect it! Expect that you will be prompted again and again by the many things you need yet to "get."

If you are in this universal flow of peace, love, joy and abundance, (and who doesn't want to be in this flow), you can expect that when you ask, you will receive! And it never, ever, shows up in the manner that you think it should. Never! I have a dear friend who has totally changed her life from one business to another, into a spiritual realm, and it's not coming out anything like she thought it would. Sometimes it is necessary for people to take their journey of change on their own, and in those circumstances I am reluctant to give them too much advice. But I can't say this enough, "It will not be what you expect, it will not be when you expect it, nor will it be from the direction you think it will come." It never does. That's because we're not working with a human mind. When we give our affairs over to God, we give up our attempt to run them ourselves. And because we are not in charge, we don't have to be in control of how everything is supposed to work out! God, unlimited Divine Energy of Love, is working behind the scenes to create synchronicity. Synchronicity is what we humans call "coincidences." Synchronicity puts you in the right place at the right time so that you can receive exactly what you need.

When you trust, everything you need is already on your path. Everything you need comes to you. I say this over and over again because it has worked in my life for the past ten years. With three businesses, where it sometimes seems like money is just going out and nothing is coming back in let me tell you, trust works! Have that trust. Put your affairs in the hands of the Divine, and the Divine will come in with love and your best interest. When everything seems chaotic, when it's not working out the way you want, that's the time you're supposed to say, "I do not resist this situation! I give it to you, God. I know it is in my best interest."

You're not going to ask God for an apple and then have Him or Her give you a snake. That won't happen. It doesn't happen, ever. It may look like a snake at first. But you will find through your trust that you are going to get the apple that you need and want in your life. You will get the apple and then some.

"I do not resist this situation."

When you let go of control of the outcome, you allow that energy to flow in your life. You allow for that Grace to come in. You allow for the love, joy, peace, and abundance that is yours by right, just because you are who you are, and because you believe and trust.

We have to work to put back the belief and trust that we came into this world possessing, because we have been sidetracked by our society which has taught us to doubt and be skeptical; to believe in only what we can see. We need to use these Eight Keys to the Kingdom just to bring to us what we should have had all along – love, joy, peace and abundance.

So our task for this chapter is to exercise the verb of trust, not for sixty seconds like we did for "Believe," but you are going to look at everything in your life, and you are going to say, "I do not resist this situation." I guarantee that when you let go and you trust, that most of the time with very little effort on your part, whatever issues you've got going will work themselves out for the highest and best good.

Sometimes we're supposed to do something. Sometimes the resolution of our issue requires action on our part. If so, we will be led, and the only way that you are going to get that information about how to be led is if you're in the moment and trusting. When you are in the moment is when God and the angels can speak to you. Only when you are in the moment can you receive the messages from them that you need to guide you to do what you need to do. So if you're all stressed about the changes and chaos in your life, and what's going to happen in the future, you are not being in the moment. And worrying about how you're going to make that mortgage payment in the next three weeks is not thinking in the moment. Allowing yourself to be drawn into negative feelings and thoughts about situations that are in the future does not allow you to be in the moment.

You know people like that – we are like that from time to time ourselves – worrying about things we have to do six weeks from now and getting all stressed about it. Six weeks is a long time away, and we live in a universe that can get an awful lot done in just sixty seconds. Think back to that first sixty-second exercise we did in "Believing." In that sixty seconds, when you totally believed, your whole life path shifted. If the angels can do that in sixty-seconds, what is six weeks to them, or a month, or a day? It can't happen unless you trust. If a synchronistic moment comes your way, if you're stressing and worrying about something else and right in front of you someone is saying, "Let me help you with this situation," you won't hear it. You won't recognize the help when it is presented.

I gave a reading for a woman years ago who came to me asking for help. She was living in a mobile home and needed someone to come into her life that would help her find a way to get a house she wanted to live in; someone who could put the whole deal together for her. She told me there was a man at her church that was willing to do the mortgage for her, but she really didn't want to bother him with it. Obviously, she wasn't thinking that what was presented to her in that moment was her gift from God. Angels come in many, many forms. Sometimes we let our ego or pride act as blinders, making us miss what's offered, thinking what we need must come more directly or in a more obvious form. This woman thought that her help needed to come from someone who didn't already know her, needed to perhaps be more anonymous, or even be a little more dramatic. She totally missed what was being presented to her.

You've all heard the story about the flood where a person is sitting on a rooftop praying to God to save them. A helicopter comes by. Then a boat comes by, each offering to take him off the roof. "No, no thank you. God is going to save me." We laugh at this joke because it is so obvious that the person did not recognize God's help. Twice! Let's not miss our help! Be in the moment and accept the gifts that are being given to you. This is trust in action.

You wouldn't think that trusting would be that hard. But we literally have to turn our belief system completely around to accommodate the gifts from God: love, peace, joy, and abundance. Isn't it weird that we have to work to replace the beliefs we once had, the ones we brought with us into this world, in order to recognize and accept the gifts from God that are intended for us, were always intended for us, and to which we have a natural right? What kind of world do we live in where we're not taught to automatically accept God's gifts? But we're not. We don't. So we have to learn how. That's what this message of the Eight Keys is all about – learning how to accept.

Trust is all about acceptance. You believed. You opened up the door. You walked through that door. Sixty seconds is all it took. Your life is on a new path, and now everything is all screwed up. Everything is different and you are scared. Now you are trusting. You accept that what you ask God to do She will do. You expect that your life will change as a result of God's help. You don't expect the changes you get. And that feels chaotic. That's when you have to trust that everything is working. And you just say: "I do not resist this situation. I give it to you, God."

I promise you – and I do not say this lightly – whatever situation you have is not too big for God. I couldn't stand up and speak before crowds of people, and I couldn't put it in writing for the world to see if I didn't know it to be true.

Nothing is too big for the Divine Energy to take care of it. Just get out of the way. And TRUST.

Meditation #2

Lean back. Take a slow deep breath and exhale, sending all your tension, doubt, and anxieties out with your breath. Do it a few more times until you feel totally relaxed.

Now from your heart chakra, the center of your chest, imagine a bright light – a warm bright light that is the energy of love within you. Let that energy grow brighter and larger, like a great bubble of light. Let it engulf you.

Right now, feel the energy. Enjoy the energy.

Trust is a verb, an action required of you. Trust that the light is love, that the energy is God. For this moment, take that action.

Let that bubble of light rise out of you. Enlarge it until it encompasses the planet and everything on it. Let the bright center of the bubble rise out of you.

No matter what that situation is in your life, no matter what is happening to you, whatever you're feeling physically, mentally, emotionally, place that issue, those feelings into that bright center of that bubble now.

You have just placed them into God's outstretched hands. You have turned them over to the experts. Trust that they will be taken care of to your best interest.

Now expect change… divine change.

And when that change comes, just trust and say: "I…do not resist…this situation."

Linda's Story: A Violation of Trust

When I was born, my mother didn't want another child. It was almost all she could do to get through her day with the one child she had. My father was a cold and emotionally disconnected husband and father who absented himself from home as much as possible, leaving his children to be raised solely by my mother. I learned at a very early age that I had little value to my mother. She interacted with me as little as possible, which resulted in me developing a very low self esteem. To my father I was nearly a non-person, except in one way. All that negative energy engulfing the family set me up to be a perfect victim for my father's sexual abuse. I want to share with you the impact this abuse had on me. I am hoping that those of you reading now who have had similar experiences will gain more understanding for yourselves.

When a trusted adult (and all adults are trusted at first), chooses this kind of behavior it wreaks havoc on a child's basic instincts. Each one of us is born psychic. These intuitive feelings run very deep. Adults are the ones we trust and rely on for our care and protection and to teach us how to make our way in the world. They are the big people and we don't expect them not to be right. When the trusted adult does things that the child knows intuitively to be so wrong, and then tells that child that it is alright, it creates such a strong conflict in the child, that those who were violated, instead of not trusting the adult, learn not to trust their intuition and to doubt themselves. It must be okay, because this person is the adult and is smarter than I. But I don't feel okay. Our child's logic tells us that because we don't feel okay, we must be the ones that are at fault. I learned this lesson so young that I had no conscious memory of when it began.

Child abuse comes in many forms, great and small. But all disturb the nature of trust that children, by instinct, must give adults in order to survive. Another simple example of a violation of trust I experienced many times as a child, and that has long lasting effects for all children with similar experience, was being told by my parents that everything was "fine," when the truth pointed to the exact opposite. When my parents did not get along, the effect was stone cold silences that often flooded the house, adding to the already cold emotional environment. All of my instincts and intuition told me this was not right. When I would ask what was wrong, I was told that everything was "fine," nothing was wrong. I didn't want to doubt my parents because they were the adults and they were supposed to know. Perhaps they just wanted to protect my sister and me from the reality of their relationship. But, more likely, they were practicing what they were taught – that what affected the adults was none of the children's business. Like a great many adults of their time, they had no concept of the life-long effects the dynamics of their relationships had on their children. This too, contributed to my growing up not trusting my intuition and doubting myself. When I became an adult I had to learn to trust myself and God, which was quite a struggle because my self esteem had been diminished to nearly zero.

By the time I was eight years old, my father, although still living in the house, had completely emotionally abandoned us. The good thing about that was that the molestations stopped. The bad thing was how painful his emotional disconnection and lack of attention was for me. It may be hard for you to understand, because his attentions upon me were wrong and made me feel incredibly conflicted. But I felt rejected and hurt when his attention stopped. At least while he was molesting me, I felt I had his love. Children need their parents' love and attention even if it is negative. All attention, to a child, translates as love. He disconnected emotionally and never came back. I felt at fault for his lack of interest. I thought I had done something terribly wrong to cause him not to love me anymore. I spent a good deal of my life trying to accept that his attention was not his love, and learning what the definition of love should be.

Still it was a big relief when my father finally left the family home. I truly thought things would be better for my sister, Mom , and me. For a while before he left, things were so stressed I could feel it in the energy of our home. Mom would have dinner ready and anxiously wait hours for Dad to come home. When he arrived, Dad would seem distracted, disinterested, and quiet. As usual, no one ever spoke about there being a problem. They didn't argue or fight, at least not in front of my sister and me. They continued to say that everything was "alright" for five more years.

I was thirteen when my father finally left. I didn't see or hear from him again until I was eighteen. And after that we rarely communicated at all. We spoke by phone a few times over the years, and the interesting part of that is that every time he called I would revert to being six years old. I would hear his voice and my heart would cry out, "Daddy!" I would gush on and on, telling him how well I was doing and all the things I had accomplished. I was determined to make him proud of me, so I became the "good" girl, the smart and capable daughter who would never dream of calling him with a problem, ever. I wanted him to love me and be my "daddy."

I would be totally drained by the end of our usually short conversation. It took me years to realize what I was doing. I would get off the phone and wonder where all that emotion came from. I was trying so hard. The real kicker of it all is that he was totally incapable of being "daddy." He wasn't trying at all. Unrealistic as it may sound, I always thought that if I were good enough he would really love me, but I had to be the one that was good enough. The reality, of course, is that I could never be good enough for him to truly love me like a daddy should, because there was never a daddy in him. It never occurred to me that he should have been the one trying to gain my love, forgiveness, and respect.

I finally came to accept how our relationship turned out because I finally realized it wasn't me. He just couldn't do the daddy thing. His life was all about him. He was a man who couldn't love and give his heart to anyone. No matter how I tried, or how good I was, or how much money I made, or how much success I had, nothing in him would change. He was who he was, and the greatest gift I ever gave him and myself, was just accepting that. The truth is I never had a "daddy" and never will. And I am okay with that.

When I finally pulled my energy away from trying to change him to just accepting him, it freed us both. We can't make people change, no matter how hard we try, or how much we love. It must come from within. However, we can change how we react to them.

It is not our job to change other people, only ourselves. So get on with it. Forget who doesn't love you and figure out a way to find value in yourself. In having this wonderful revelation, I was finally able to talk to my father without reverting to being a six-year old. I released all expectations for him and our relationship.

While I was writing this book, I found out that Dad had developed a major heart condition. Trouble with the physical heart is the extension of emotional heart issues. Blockages in his heart valves equate to blockages with his ability to love. We manifest in our physical bodies what we hold in our emotional bodies. These two cannot be disconnected.

Growing up in such circumstances makes abuse victims very creative children. We come up with survival mechanisms to get through the trauma that we carry within us our whole lives. I am amazed by the number of adults that come to me for therapy who still react to life based on the survival techniques they created as children. Of course I did too, well into my own adulthood. I am happy to say, through my own journey of self-discovery, I no longer feel the need for these techniques, which was one of the reasons the angels prompted me to write this book.

Just a few of the more common survival techniques include: being able to leave your body by astral traveling, or emotionally "checking out" during stressful times; selectively remembering traumatic events, or not remembering them at all; being a compulsively "good" child, even in adulthood; becoming an over achiever or overdoing for people to avoid making anyone upset; becoming the caregiver, and feeling responsible for the well being of those around you; being the comedian in the family, class, or community to get attention even when that behavior irritates people; getting sick when you feel stress, or in order to avoid dealing with unpleasant situations. There are many, many more. The point of knowing which ones you use is to learn more positive ways to cope and to get past the reasons for needing the techniques. Think about how you react in your family dynamics or when drama comes up in your life. The very frightened child in you will take over by putting one or more survival techniques into action.

Learning to trust can be difficult, but not at all impossible, even for the victims of abuse. It starts with a desire for a better way to get through your life. It depends upon believing you can have that better way. It gets stronger as you learn that you deserve this better way, that you are worthy just because you were born, not because of anything you did, or didn't do, or will do, because the Spirit of the Divine resides within you. It flourishes when you accept that God and the angels are offering that better way to you with no strings attached. It always was, is now, and always will be, yours already. And that you can trust.

Divorce American Style

In 1967 divorce was not very common. So it was a huge stigma for us to be the only divorced family we knew. Although none of our friends or family made a point of mentioning our "predicament," we were the black sheep and I felt it, whether at school, in family gatherings, or out in the neighborhood. Our neighborhood was typical of the mid-twentieth century middle class American dream – identical houses huddled closely together; the elementary school in walking distance just around the block, with the same friendly crossing guard for all the years I attended. And we knew all the neighbors for blocks around. But that was where the similarity to "typical" ended.

I was in junior high school by the time the divorce papers came to our house. I will never forget that day. The idea that maybe things might be better after my father left went right out the window. My sister and I got off the bus and walked down Longview Avenue to our home at 18818. The drapes were closed and the house was dark. Mom was sitting in the chair crying, holding her newly received divorce papers. In her other hand was a bottle of pills. I don't know what they were, but I believed her when she said she wanted to kill herself. I really thought she would do it. My sister and I didn't know what to do. We started to cry, got on our knees and begged her not to do it, not to leave us alone. But we weren't persuading her.

We were able, however, to persuade our father after some tearful begging, to come and talk to her. I don't know what he said to her. But I remember he smoked and coughed a lot, like he was choking on his own words. He didn't stay long, and after he left Mom seemed to calm down. She put the pills away and promised that for our sakes, she would not kill herself. She kept her word and never threatened suicide again. With denial steeped deeply into our bones from years of practice, the next day Nancy and I went to school as if nothing had ever happened, and I prayed for a good hair day. I felt ugly, out of place, with no confidence in myself. That was a feeling I knew well, and still occasionally lurks around the corner of my consciousness.

That first summer on our own was genuinely weird. Mom developed phobias for everything. She couldn't function in the outside world. The drapes were always closed and the house always dark. Nancy and I stayed in with her. We had no life, no friends, only a threatened sense of survival in the little house at 18818. Mom had never been on her own, had no education or training, and was scared to death. By the end of the summer she had found some courage and decided to enter the world again. She said she did it for us, because she saw that we were being dragged down the path of darkness with her. She decided to find work. This was not a simple task for a divorced woman that had never had a job. And getting a well paying job in 1967 was difficult for any woman. The women's movement was very new, and they were just starting to get inspired to burn their bras. Mom was hired for one of the limited jobs available at that time for unskilled women – a phone solicitor. It was not a glamorous job. But she was earning a paycheck and began feeling pretty good about herself.

For a few years she kept it together. And during that time I remember that she was calmer and it seemed easier for her to show Nancy and me how much she loved us. During that time she and I grew very close, and there were moments when we seemed to connect so completely at the heart level. She seemed a very wise woman to me, knowing the right things to say to make me feel better about myself and answering my questions honestly and openly. Although she remained confused, scattered, and unable to make a decision about her own issues for most of the rest of her life, she had the uncanny ability to focus on me and offer amazing wisdom that still comes to mind when I need it, even now.

I remember one time sitting at her feet when I was around sixteen or seventeen-years old. I was telling her about a problem I was having with a boyfriend. She looked at me and said earnestly, but quietly, "Never, ever, ever, play second best to anybody." I know I didn't totally grasp her meaning at that time because I had absolutely no self esteem whatsoever. But years later her words would come back to me at a time when the meaning became very clear, and I fully appreciated what she meant.

During these few years she actually seemed to be having fun, and seemed to be able to push her troubling thoughts to the side. She dated, had friends, and looked awesome. She made men turn their heads. This didn't last, but it is a time I will never forget because we would laugh a lot. I remember our laughter.

One of the many things I have learned over the years is that the woman of the household holds the energy for the family. She is like the center of the wheel and everyone else revolves around her. If she has fear, it will spread to the family like a disease. When she is happy and content, the family will also mirror that energy and be more relaxed. For all you moms out there, take note. You cannot afford to neglect yourselves. The most important job you have is to make sure you are getting what you need, whether it is sleep, exercise, or just some quiet time. I emphasize this, because when my mom began to feel better about herself, my sister and I felt better about ourselves as well.

A Family Legacy

Mom grew up in a family of Hungarian immigrants surrounded by friends and family that were also immigrants. Everyone had a story of some relative, grandfather, grandmother, uncle, who came over on "The Boat." It was always just referred to as "The Boat." They never explained which boat, but I guess that was not the point. Everyone would nod and smile when someone spoke of "The Boat." Some of my earliest memories are of stories of how Mom's parents came over from Hungary with their parents, and somehow they ended up in Cleveland, Ohio. Cleveland was very ethnic, each of the different nationalities banded together to make their own quaint little neighborhoods. Each neighborhood was a small cultural expression of the immigrant's home towns. They may have come to the "new world" to change their lives but being human, many brought their "old world" issues, problems, and cultural mores with them.

My mother's family was no different. Mom's parents, much to their shame, got married because Grandma was pregnant with my mom. You just didn't do that in the 1920s, at least not according to my grandmother. In fact, "having to get married," as it was termed, remained a stigma in the mainstream of American culture well into the 1980s. I don't think Grandma ever forgave her daughter for coming when she did. Mom paid for that her whole life. Grandma did have another child, a son, the "apple of her eye." And she never hesitated to say so.

My mother told me of how beatings and sexual abuse were the norm in her childhood. Beatings for being born too soon and also, I believe, for being the subject of grandpa's sexual attention. It is no wonder why Mom couldn't wait to get out of her parent's house, away from the hatred and abuse. When my father entered the picture, and it turned out that grandpa hated him, Mom grabbed the opportunity to marry him.

Mom was a manic depressive, with obsessive-compulsive behavior. For those of you who have OCD, are manic depressive, or bipolar as they call it now, or if you live with someone with OCD, you understand the difficulties. There is so much more that can be done these days to help with these conditions. However, in the late 50s and early 60s there weren't many options. And then, to add insult to injury, each of the three psychiatrists Mom saw in her life died in the middle of her therapy. Try to fight irony that dark!

Over the years, Mom's doctors prescribed many different drugs. One of the first was Dexedrine Elixir, commonly referred to as "Speed" on the streets. She would have a big bottle tucked away and when she got depressed, she would go to the cupboard and take a swig, a little lift for Mom. Then at night, "downers" would help her sleep – all legally supplied. None of the drugs helped her get over the issues she had from childhood, or helped her out of her depression, but it seemed to be the treatment of choice by her many doctors. During my mid to late teens, when things seemed to get better, she didn't seem to need so much of the meds. She just seemed to be happier.

By the time I was in my first year of college, Mom had met a man that she would later marry. When she met him she was feeling pretty good and had become quite independent. But some people are deeply imprinted as victims, and you just can't get rid of that imprint easily. The abusers can pick the victims out a mile away and zero in on them. Mom had that imprint. He wined and dined her, gave her gifts, made her feel special. What a wonderful man. They moved in together and he finally talked her into getting married. When she was again in a position of total dependency, everything changed and the abuse started. It wasn't physical abuse. This man was a controlling despot. He ruled her with absolute power, oppressing her spirit over the next twenty years until there was little left of who she really could have been.

One of the last times Mom and I were together, we were able to spend some real quality time. Although she rarely talked about the unpleasant portions of her life, she shared with me the condition of her life with her husband. Then she talked about her relationship with her mother. And what she said came as quite a surprise to me. Mom told me that all she really ever wanted was for her mother to love her. Her mother never told her she loved her. Mom shared a story of how one time when she was a little girl, she asked her mother if she loved her. Grandma's response was, "Why? Do you want something?"

Mom spent her whole life trying to get her mother to love her. As she was telling me this, she was crying, just like a little girl – a little girl that never got love. At that time there wasn't much I could say or do to help her with that overwhelming grief that engulfed her. I just held her, understanding so much more than I did before. My mother died taking care of her mother. A massive heart attack ended her life.

Her heart just broke. She couldn't take it anymore. She never did hear those precious words "I love you" from her mother.

These are the wounded people who raised me, my mother and my father, who passed on their legacy to me. It was truly up to me to take what they gave me, their strengths, their weaknesses, and whatever characteristics of my own that came with me at birth, and run the gauntlet of this life. Yes, we pick our parents and create our circumstances for the opportunity of enlightenment. Believe me there have been many times over the years that I really wished I could see that contract because I couldn't believe what I agreed to. It is up to each of us to take our circumstances and use them to propel ourselves forward. And from a legacy like this, one must believe and trust that the leap forward into enlightenment will be like a cannon shot!

Third Key: Detachment

So far in our series, we have discussed the keys of "Believe" and "Trust." Our first Key to the Kingdom is to be able to believe that we can actually have the Kingdom of Heaven on Earth. We need to open up that door. That's the purpose of believing, and it's why it's the first key. Take a moment right now and put aside everything you think is your reality. Allow yourself to believe that God didn't just dump you here on this planet without any guidance, without any hope, or without any joy. It is your right to have that guidance, hope, and joy, and the way to tap into it is to believe! Let that be the first thing you do, the first Key you make your own.

With the Key of Belief firmly in your grip, you have opened up the door to all kinds of possibilities. The next step is to begin exercising the verb of "Trust." You have to trust that God is really watching over you, that God is going to take care of you. Remember, in the last chapter I told you that no one can screw up your life the way God can? That the chaos in your life is merely the changes you asked for?

When you set out to change your life, to believe, to trust, to say, "Okay, God, I am ready for the higher energy, I am ready to step into a life of joy, I am ready to step into a life of abundance, I am ready to step into a life of health," you need to be prepared that God is going to make some changes. You can't keep going down the same path you were before, because, if it had been working, if that path had brought you what you needed, you wouldn't have anything to change. And change always screws us up! There isn't one of us that don't have a moment of terror when our life isn't going to be the same after today. I don't care what direction we're heading, change always gets to us. This is why trust is so important, and why it is the second Key.

We humans are just beginning to understand that our thoughts create. Comprehending this actually introduces us to the four dimensional world of quantum physics! We determine our own futures by what we expect them to be. So, we are actually creatures with four dimensional minds, living in what heretofore, was said to be a three dimensional world. However, we still think we can't see into the future and we want to know what's going to happen tomorrow.

So many of us are like a client that came to me for an angel reading who said, "I'm just frustrated because I don't know what

I'm doing. I don't know where I'm going. I don't know what job I'm going to get. I don't know where I'm going to live in a year. I don't know what's going to happen to me." My answer to her was, "Well, neither do I."

Do you really think that anybody is actually going to step up and tell you what's going to happen, detail for detail? Let's say they did. Let's say we could put it in stone, "Here's what's going to happen, here's where you are going, here's your job, this is where you will be living in a year. Here's the manuscript of your life, these are the steps you're going to take. This is what your life will be." Could anything possibly be more boring? Where's the spice in life? Where is the excitement? Where's the option to move even higher than this? Why would you even want to put that limit on yourself? There is nothing consistent in the universe except change. If you are fighting against change right now you must be making yourself miserable. You have to be, because you're totally going against the flow. Put that Key of Trust into action, now.

With both the Key of Belief and the Key of Trust engaged, let's move a step further to the Key of Detachment.

As I tried to prepare for the presentation of each Key, as much as the angels would allow me to prepare, I would think, "Oh, this is the most important one!" When I was preparing for "Believe," I couldn't think of how anything could be more important, until "Trust" came along. Now with the Key of Detachment it's, "Oh no, this is the most important one!" Well, you need all of the Keys. Each Key only unlocks a portion of what you need to bring Heaven into your life. Now the angels want you to have the Key of Detachment.

What could that possibly mean: "Detachment?"

Detachment is also a verb, the act of letting go. This may come as a shock to some of you, but to detach you must let go of control! Believe it or not, you have never really had control over anything anyway. The sooner you get used to that, the more peaceful you're going to be. Detaching from the outcome is the best and greatest gift you can give to yourself. Quit wringing your hands! Quit worrying! Put that energy into trust, put trust into action, and let go.

Here's why letting go is vital: Because you don't want to mess with the flow. Your good is coming to you; it is already on its way. And it makes it more difficult to get to you when you're pushing and shoving and working, working, working to make things happen.

You've got a plan and you are determined to make it work! Well, you know what they say about plans? I've said it before, and I'll say it again: if you want to make God laugh, show Him your plan!

When you have your whole life planned out and set in stone as to how it is going to be, not only is it boring, but you miss out on all the fun! You miss out on the excitement of discovering something beyond just what you see. Detaching allows you to say, "I have no control and that's okay. It's okay not to control this situation." We need to let go, because in letting go we are actually saying that we are trusting God to create for us the best path available. And that we are willing to accept that path. People think that knowing what their future is will release them from worry, that knowing what is going to happen gives them an "out." What you don't realize, is that you don't have to worry anyway!

As I said before, God did not just dump us here on this earth. You have an intuitive psychic ability, right in your heart center, that guides you where you need to go, let's you know what's going to happen to you, and tells you how it will happen. Every single one of us has it, not just "special" people. I have it and just happen to use it for a living. So I practice it all the time. Yours just needs practice too. The problem is, if you don't detach, if you're wringing your hands worrying all the time, you can't hear it. Most of us are so busy all day, thoughts constantly running through our heads about what we need to do, that we don't even give ourselves quiet time to reflect on what's going on around us. What we do is wait until we are trying to go to sleep at night. But that's when our heads fill with what we didn't do that day, and we worry about the future consequences.

A good example of a lost opportunity for detachment is when we're driving in our car. Before cell phones, I would do my best thinking in my car because my brain had a captive audience. And to add to that distraction, the cell phone has given us the ability to act on those thoughts, to call our office, or our kids, or our next appointment, to keep in touch or to give instructions, and to keep tabs on stuff we probably can't do anything about until we get there anyway. We sit in our cars and our heads spin like hamsters on a wheel. That is not being detached. Do you really think that if God or the angels even showed up in the seat next to you that you might even notice? Do you think you could even hear another voice speaking to you, even if that voice was God's?

Well, of course not! Because you are human and you are trying to figure out your life, trying to find solutions to situations, trying to do the best you can to take care of what needs taking care of. There is one tremendous discrepancy with that. You are trying to figure things out in human terms, which prevents you from tapping into this incredible source working behind the scenes, trying to take care of all the issues you asked that Source to handle. When you detach – let go of control, really give it to God and let your mind go, "Ahhh," – you can get the guidance you need and the help you asked for.

We hear stories all the time about people who are in the right place at the right time, meeting up, synchronicity, coincidences. But we always seem to hear it happening to other people. Do you want to see it happen in your own life? Then begin detaching. Let go. Let go of your emotional commitment to saving the soul of that person you feel needs to be saved in one way or another. Detach from that financial situation that has you locked in its barrel sites. Detach from that health situation that has you under its control because you know your body is trying to tell you something. Open up to the message and the messenger that has been trying to give it to you! The universe is unlimited. Therefore, there are infinite solutions. But you don't know about them until you let that messenger bring you that message.

Letting go of control is to let go of fear. And fear is no way to live your life. Our society would love to keep us all tangled up and wrapped up in fear. I saw a commercial the other day where a little boy was sitting at a kitchen counter eating a sandwich. The announcer was saying, "Now, you wouldn't let your children eat their food in the mud! Well, there are three billion bacteria on your countertop!" The sole purpose of that ad was to make you very, very afraid, so you will buy their bacteria killing product. That's just one small thing to keep you afraid. God doesn't want you to be afraid! The Spirit of Divine Love never set up this program of fear! Fear is used so that people can keep control of you! There is nothing to be afraid of. God is taking care of you. The sooner you detach from the ways of the world and the emotional commitment that you have to situations, the sooner you can get out from under the control of fear!

"Oh, Linda, that's so hard, though! Especially when it's someone you love." I hear you. I hear this all the time. I lived it. I sometimes still live it. It's difficult. I'm not saying it's easy. Nothing worthwhile is ever easy. Detaching is no exception. To put it simply, what you're really dealing with is a habit of the way you react to life. It's just a habit. And habits can be changed. Anybody ever quit smoking? I did. It was difficult. Anybody miss smoking? I did in the beginning. There are many people who don't make it the first time they try to quit. But the people who successfully kicked that habit did not want to go back, so the effort was worth it! The effort to quit worrying and the effort to get out of fear is also worth it!

So how do you do that? You do it by changing your thoughts. When you feel fear rising, or feel like things will never get better, you remind yourself that you believe. You believe that you can conquer fear. You believe that the Love Energy of the Universe is taking care of you, that the situation will be resolved. You believe that things will get better. Then, you begin the act of trusting. And you detach. You say, "Okay angels. Okay God. I'm giving this to you."

I am sure you will have to do that a hundred times the first day you decide to break the fear habit, because it's going to keep popping up in your mind just like that hamster on the wheel. But every time you start worrying about that loved one, or about the business, or begin worrying about anything you've got going in your life, say:

"Take this from me. Take care of the situation, and take care of my fear. God, handle this."

Then let it go...a hundred times, maybe a hundred and fifty, maybe even two hundred times, the first day. But it's worth it and you're breaking a habit. And what you are doing is detaching. You have to detach, to let go, in order for the communication that you deserve, and which is already there for you, to come to you.

How do you let go of someone you love? How do you detach from what's happening to them? You have to use your Key of Trust. Do you think that your worry is going to accomplish anything? Think about it. Do you really think that your worry will change anything in the situation that has you worried? The truth is, if it did, no one would have to tell you to let go of your worrying. You cannot possibly come up with an answer to your situation that will make it any better. You can't, because you don't know what is going on. You do not know all of the details. God knows all the details, the angels know, and they are working behind the scenes. The more you push and shove to make something happen, the harder it gets and the more the universe seems to push you right back.

I don't care what it is that you want to accomplish in your life, if you believe, and you trust, and you detach, it will come together.

But here is a fact that I can't stress often enough: It will never come together in the manner in which you think it should. God does not work in the same way that we do. Thank goodness for that! Be glad, because now your possibilities are endless instead of being limited to even this 4-D mind that we now understand that we have!

Detach from your expectations of what the outcome should be. Let it go. And suddenly you're at peace.

Now watch. Watch your good come to you. Watch these situations get taken care of. There's always an answer out there! How it's taken care of is Divine. There is an incredible tapestry that's being woven on the other side. God said, "I'm going to take care of all this for you. I can handle this. I am the big Kahuna!"

So why would you want to worry? Why would you want to do that to yourself? Do you know what stress does to the body? It's a total deterioration. When you are under stress, the adrenal glands send adrenalin rushing to all the organs, putting them into hyper action, as if the body is in fear and needs to flee. The thyroid gets screwed up. The heart starts pounding faster. The muscles tense to make ready for an action that never comes. All of this, over time, has devastating negative effects on every organ in the body. If you stay under stress long enough, your sympathetic nervous systems just stay on! It never goes off again. Can't sit down, can't relax. In my practice I see people like that all the time. By the time they make it to me for the therapies I have to offer, they are completely overcome with the effects of stress and are at their last resort.

So let it go! That's what detachment is all about. Let everything in your body go, "Aahh." Give your stress over to God and the angels, and by the end of twenty-eight days you will have a new habit of detachment. No matter how many times you have to make that conscious effort that first day, I assure you, by the next day you'll only have to do it a fraction of that many. And each day after, you'll have to do it less and less.

Wayne Dyer has a book, *Ten Secrets of Success and Inner Peace*. It's a wonderful little "puffy" book made to be given as a gift. The first time I opened this little book I read up to the first secret and never got to the other nine, because I was so impressed with that one. It said, "Expect everything and attach to nothing." Even Deepak Chopra writes about detachment in his book *The Seven Spiritual Laws*.

Expect everything to be taken care of and let go of your expectations for how it should be done. Let go of your need to worry, stress, or control, and do not expect that you can affect the outcome. Detach! Let...it...go!

Worry is a negative energy. And why would you want to put more negative energy into an already negative situation. What good does that do? It's like trying to put a fire out with gasoline! Detaching gives you space to surround the issue with positive energy, with God's love, with angels, white light, or pink light. Do it. And then release it. Believe it or not, you don't have to save that other person! Believe it or not, your mission is not for total self-sacrifice and poverty. That's not the way God has meant for us to live. You do not have to take that path.

I'll make this a quick story, because you can read the details in another chapter, but it really does emphasize how we get stuck like that hamster on a wheel. Detachment was a huge lesson for me to learn. There was a two year period when I was renting space for my office. In that period of two years I moved my office four times.

It was through no fault of my own – one owner sold the building, another raised the rent; the next brought in a bigger business. It was just circumstances. By the fourth time I was really tired, and told the angels that I wanted to have an office of my own where nobody could throw me out, and I wouldn't have to be under anyone else's control. So, of course, I made a plan. I felt that the only way that I could get what I wanted was to have my office in my home. And the only way I could have my office in my home was to sell the house and move into town. Oh, can you see how this just gets bigger and bigger?

I spent a year and a half of renovating and trying to sell my house. In all that time, no one made us an offer. Nobody even came to see it! You would think that, maybe, sometime during that year and a half, it might have occurred to me that I was possibly on the wrong path! But I had a mindset. Do you know how bad a mindset can be? The only way I could visualize getting an office of my own was by my plan. It took me a year and a half of frustration and stress until I finally realized that my plan wasn't working! All that pushing and shoving to get my plan done and the renovation of the house we ended up with didn't even include the office space that started the whole thing in the first place!

Then, after I finally admitted that my efforts were not working, I was informed that the store from which I had been working was closing, and I would have to find new space. I couldn't believe it.

I had to move again! Just when I thought things couldn't be more disappointing, a remarkable thing happened. Out of the blue, an unexpected opportunity to run a store of my own came into my hands. Soon after, a space became available that I also did not expect! Everything happened so fast! I had less than two weeks to put together a new business at a new location! When all the dust settled, I realized that I had gotten exactly what I had asked for...everything, including an office! Nobody could take my store away, they couldn't take my office away, and none of it happened the way I thought it would. I kept my life on hold for a year and a half trying to force a situation to happen. The Divine Energy just said, "Okay, we'll wait this out. She'll get it. She's a little slow, but she'll get it."

In the end, I received everything I asked for, but not until I quit obsessing and let God take care of my request. Obsession is insisting a situation has to work a certain way! God usually wants it to work Her way. If I had detached from it in the beginning I would have known sooner that my plan would not work out because God would have said, "Oh, by the way, here's a good idea for you." And it would have come to me the same way that it did a year and a half later when I was finally forced to say, "Well, maybe I'm not on the right track here."

The angels tell me that the path is supposed to be simple and it's supposed to be easy. If it's not simple and easy you're doing something wrong. If you're interfering, if you're messing with the flow, if you're not communicating, you're not getting your Divine guidance, because it's supposed to be easy. If you're hitting up against a brick wall, back off! Get your face away from the bricks so you can actually see what's going on. God is offering you support and guidance every single minute of every single day. And when you detach from the outcome you can see it more clearly. If I had been emotionally detached from the outcome of my request for office space of my own, I would have never sat around for a year and a half making myself miserable and forcing a situation that was not divine.

My plan did not work because it had nothing to do with the divine plan. There is no way for us to know the divine plan, unless and until we accept the possibility of one. Once we let go of our need to control and admit that we don't have the means to imagine all of the infinite ways that God can resolve our issues, the divine plan can be revealed to us as it is implemented. When you detach from the outcome, God takes care of the details. God will take care of that person you are concerned about. God will take care of the financial burden that is getting you down. God will take care of whatever you give Her to handle. The path is unlimited. But first you have to let go.

"Expect everything and attach to nothing."

I am never going to forget that lesson in detachment. And I hope I'm never that obsessed again with "my plan." Thankfully, I'm not as bad as I used to be. Now it only takes me a couple of weeks to see the error of my thinking and to let go. But seriously, now I say to God, "Okay, if you want this to happen then you're going to have to make it happen. If you want me to do this, or you want me to go here, or you want me to go there, then you're going to have to give me the means," and She does. When She instructs me to take action, She gives me the capability of completing that action. She wanted me to stand up and talk at Unity Church every other Sunday for three months, and She made it easy by giving me the message. She said, "Write a book. Get it out to the public." And She sent me the people that could make it happen." The Divine Energy does this, and it did this, and it always will.

God wants the process to be simple and easy, so it's joyful, so you are light of heart. Life should be joyful. Your relationship with your family and friends should be joyful. When you detach, it will be. When you figure out that you don't need any person's approval, you will have joyful relationships. Ask for joy, then detach from how you think you should receive it. It will happen. Don't hold on to anything emotionally. God will take care of it. The big picture comes out so much better when you just let it go. That was what happened when all the dust settled and I looked around me, and I had a store and an office. Everything was better than I could have ever imagined.

Detach! Do you really want to know all the details of what is going to happen to you? If you did, it would most likely frighten you out of doing what you want to do. It would overwhelm you to know how far you can go, how great you can be, how wonderful your life could become. Let that be exciting!

There was a lady who first taught me energy work, who asked me during a treatment/training session, "Do you want me to tell you what you're going to be doing?" I thought for a minute, and as anxious as I was to know, I answered, "I definitely don't want to know." I knew it would be overwhelming. The mystery, the excitement; the fact that you're not stuck to a list of things that have to happen in your life – that's the joy. Life is full of change. That's what's good about it! Detach from needing to know. Detach from the outcome of how or when it's going to happen.

Don't tell the angels how to do it! Trust them! See the end results and let them take care of the details. Let the angels, let God take care of the details. They're really good at that. They're the detail people!

Meditation #3

In this meditation, take yourself to a very peaceful place. This is your place, where no relatives, no business, nothing interferes. Nothing interferes in this very peaceful place of yours.

Picture yourself taking off the big heavy backpack, hopefully for the last time, because you are totally detaching from the outcome of your life, of your emotions, of your financial situation, and of your health, knowing that you are being cared for and watched over by God himself. Ask the angels to show up to take the backpack. And just let go.

You believe you are in a state of peace, love, joy and abundance. You are trusting. And now you're just letting go. "You take care of it, God. I'm detaching from all emotion to all of this."

Take a minute and let yourself completely detach.

You are free. Claim your freedom. Claim the promise, "It's supposed to be simple, it's supposed to be easy." Emphasize simple and easy as part of the natural flow of how your life should be: Joyful and full of not just happiness, fleeting happiness, but joy.

Tell yourself: "I accept, God. I detach from all outcomes because it's always for my best and highest good. And I allow the joy of believing and trusting the truth of this to fill me."

Now just let go.

Linda's Story: Life is Just a Trip

I left home after graduating from high school to go to college. A few months into the second year, my father's promised tuition money no longer materialized. In spite of the grants and loans I had received, I found myself out of college and headed for Columbus, Ohio, following a boyfriend who was in school there. Although the boyfriend didn't last, that adventure took me into the world of low paying jobs and shabby apartments. It didn't matter to me though, because I was young, energetic, and life was one big adventure.

Unfortunately, I took with me my victim mentality, and my skewed understanding of how relationships work, learned from my family. It must have been written across my forehead in capital letters, because I seemed to be a magnet for marginal relationships with friends, teachers, and employers that teetered continually on mutual disappointment and failure. Stumbling although I might have been, my youthful enthusiasm pulled me along, with perpetual hope that life would improve with the next adventure.

And that next adventure introduced me to Tim, the man who would become my first husband. As I look back on it now, I can say I married a man exactly like my father. I was determined that he would love me and see my value the way my father never had. I was in my early twenties when we married. And when it ended, nine years later, my efforts had no success – he didn't love me. I spent our years together allowing him to control me, hoping that would do the trick. Giving my power away was easy because I had never thought that I had any to start with. I accepted his continual criticism of me because I thought he was right. Despite the attraction he had for me in the beginning, after we married he was never satisfied with the way I dressed or the way I looked. He found an easy target in me to lay blame for anything that made him unhappy, and of course, I could never say the right thing to make up for my faults.

My life up to that point had been a series of accepting less than what I felt I was worth. And many times I would set myself up for more devaluation. Because Tim never volunteered, there were times I just had to ask him if he loved me. His usual answer was an apathetic shot back, "Sometimes." But still I continued to ask.

I hung on to nothing, thinking it would become something if I could only try hard enough, if I could love enough, or if I could somehow be better. I changed more times than the wind in those nine years, trying to make him find me valuable, trying to be worthy of his love. But Tim could only reflect back to me how I felt about myself. I learned, many years later, that we are our own benefactors. We give ourselves exactly what we think we should have. Tim didn't value me because I didn't value me. Tim couldn't love me, because I couldn't love myself.

During that marriage, my health became an issue. I had developed asthma and seemed to constantly be suffering from shortness of breath, aggravated by colds and flu. As our relationship became more stressful, breathing became more difficult and I found I could not easily walk from one end of the room to the other. One winter, my illness required hospitalization for breathing treatments. I had lost a great deal of weight and was on several medications.

Winter was particularly hard on my condition, and with each spring's warmer weather I would begin to feel better. I was convinced that it was the weather that made me sick, and one warm day I became determined not to spend another winter in the cold. I know now that it was the stress I put myself under in my marriage that was making me sick. But back then I was saying little silent prayers to get out of the cold.

Shortly after my decision to get and stay warm, Tim and I got an invitation from my sister, Nancy, to move to Arizona with her. Tim declined the offer, but I accepted, more than ready to venture out of the cold Ohio winters into the heat of the southwest. So, with new-found excitement for life, I set my mind to make that change work. I said my goodbyes and left Tim in Ohio, and so was quite surprised to have him show up on my Phoenix doorstep about a month later. That made me certain that he actually loved me. At last, I was happy, warm, and felt loved. Life was good.

We set up our lives in Phoenix and my health began to improve. But as time went on the medications weren't working that well any more and I seemed to get worse, needing more and different medications. I was building up a tolerance to the asthma medication and found that I had also become hypoglycemic. Hypoglycemia is what happens when lunch consists of candy bars and soda and chocolate as a main addiction. The years of not eating right, medication, and constant stress finally got the better of me.

I suddenly felt fed up with all the medication, the doctors, and the sickness! They weren't helping me. I decided to take the initiative to teach myself what I needed to know to get better. I began reading books from health food stores, began learning about vitamins, and herbs, and sugar, and asthma, and hypoglycemia. I learned that hypoglycemia was making my asthma worse, and that the blood sugar problem could lead to diabetes if left untreated. I learned how vitamins could have a positive effect on my conditions, and I began taking those that would help me. Soon, my poor depressed immune system began bouncing back. And as my health improved, so did my self esteem.

I see now that the angels were leading me. This was the beginning of my journey to taking responsibility for everything that happens in my life. It was the first steps away from being a "victim," although it would be years before I would release that energy completely.

The first few years in Phoenix were good ones for Tim and me. He worked nights and I worked days, and we definitely got along better when we didn't see each other too much. But, change being the only constant in the universe, change caught up with us.

Through friends who had moved to the mountains of eastern Arizona, Tim and I fell in love with one of the small towns there and became obsessed with living there. My heart ached to be in that beautiful mountain community. So we moved again. Now, after years of acknowledging the angels' work in my life, I recognize that it was they who compelled me to live there.

Life in a small community can be very difficult, especially trying to make a living, and many who come here end up leaving for that reason. But with hard work and fate on our side, Tim and I managed. Finding a permanent place to live was one of the difficulties. In such a small town, available homes are scarce. Most people must buy a lot and build. That's exactly what we did. On our small budget we could only afford to have a shell of a house built, and we planned to finish it while living there. It was like camping full time – not the best environment to improve a shaky relationship. This adventure was the straw that broke the back of our marriage, and once again change came into my life. In truth, Tim left me. He found someone else that suited his needs better. Although, when he left I was devastated, in time I realized how much better I felt without him.

When I learned about the contracts we set up for ourselves before we come to this planet, I also learned that when we understand a lesson intended by that contract, we can move on. So here was one of my lessons. I spent nine years with a man I had to convince to love me; nothing I did was good enough. When it was over I was resolved to never do that to myself again. I decided that I deserved to have someone who would love and adore me just the way I was, someone tall and handsome, and who would think me the best thing that could ever happen to him. I convinced myself that he was out there just waiting for me.

This was a completely new way of thinking for me and made me feel strangely empowered. It was my first real lesson in creating my own reality, my first exercise in dealing with the positive powers of the universe. Instead of waiting for life to beat me around as I had always done, I made a positive move toward manifesting what I wanted from God. I didn't know that was what I was doing. I was just determined not to repeat the same scenario I had with Tim. Slowly but surely, without being aware of it, I was releasing the victim living within me.

I was also not aware that with the changes in my attitude toward myself, the angels had begun weaving a very special tapestry just for me. That tapestry included a very special someone just for me. I had gotten into most of my relationships in the past because I was looking for someone to rescue me, to save the victim in me. I had chosen, what I thought subconsciously, to be strong people. But I had actually picked dominant personalities, and that just made me vulnerable to their need to control. I had reached a point where I no longer felt I needed to be rescued. Scott came into my life as I was first discovering this about myself. The angels found a person for me that matched, to a tee, the one I had described to them. He was tall and handsome and he loved and adored me. I felt freer with him than I ever did without him. He not only accepted me, all my foibles and flaws, he honored me. He saw in me qualities that I didn't even know I had. Scott became and remains, my best friend, my staunchest supporter, my biggest fan, and the place I go for renewal. He is my knight in shining armor who, instead of feeling that I need rescuing, encourages and nurtures my independence.

Yes, even with that contract, it's all about choice. And I made the choice to understand the lessons offered by that contract, to detach emotionally from them and to move on. I chose to see myself in a new light that offered possibilities which had never occurred to me before, and to accept the new path the angels had laid in front of me.

Intuitively, I had listened to the wonderful voice of my angels who said to me, "This is what you asked for. Accept the opportunities that this one-in-a-million life has to offer. Don't let them pass you by."

None of those changes could have come into my life if I had not detached from my previous expectations. I had expected to remain in an unhappy relationship, desperate to find value in myself and in my future. I finally understood that only I could change that for myself and detached from that desperation. I had expected that my medical conditions would get better by changing my geography. But I found that moving from one end of the country to the other was not as effective as understanding where my negative emotions were taking me. When I began to release some of those negative expectations, I began to get better.

Most changes don't happen overnight, and mine certainly didn't either. My self esteem was growing, but in baby steps. It would be quite a while, and many of those contract lessons later, before I would be able to move on from the effects of some of those conditions I had chosen for myself in my life contract.

Fire on the Mountain

June of 2002 was the summer that brought terror to our White Mountains; terror in the form of the Rodeo-Chediski Fire. Living surrounded by national forest in the dry southwest has always been risky, but that summer brought the added danger of a drought that had lasted several years. We had been very lucky for many years not to have had serious fire threats, but suddenly the national forest surrounding our town was aflame. Nearly a half million acres would burn, over four hundred homes would be destroyed, and more than thirty thousand people would be evacuated before that monster would be contained. There was nothing we who loved the mountain and the forests could do but wait. And we waited a very long twenty days and nights for the world as we knew it to end.

The fire was discovered on a Tuesday, and by that evening about seven hundred acres had burned. The drought had left everything incredibly dry and parched. By the next day the fire had spread over fifty thousand acres and the officials were evacuating the outlying communities. By Saturday it was our turn to get out. Even though we had been facing the probability all week, it was still a shock when we were ordered to leave. Some people had already gone, but many others would not leave. My family and I were faced with a decision of what to do. My husband, Scott, said he was going to stay to watch over our home and told me to take Jessie and go. I calmly told him, "Over my dead body. We go together, or we stay together, but we will be together no matter what." He relented, and that night we all packed.

How do you pack for an evacuation knowing everything you leave behind will be destroyed? You can't take everything, so how do you decide what to take? How do you fit everything you feel is important into your car? This was not like the times when I was college age, packing my car and moving on a whim. The simple truth was that my life had changed so much since those days I found it nearly impossible to even think about leaving. The thought of never seeing our home again was overwhelming. I just began gathering items, starting with pictures, computers, jewelry, and all our important papers, mostly basic stuff. As I sorted through our things, what to take, what to leave, priorities began coming clear. Of course we would take our pets, both our automobiles, and our RV. We could stay in the RV when we got to where we were going, wherever that might be.

I wondered how we would get our cats to cooperate with us and get into their crates when it was time. They are not like the average house cats, content to stay indoors in the lap of luxury. Our kitties liked to wander around our remote neighborhood, meandering at their leisure in the wilderness, sometimes for days. I thought what a small miracle it was that all three were home the night we got notice to leave. I feel that animals sense more things than we think they do.

The call to evacuate came at 9 P.M., and by the time we packed it was pretty late. We made the decision to stay the rest of that night and to leave in the morning. Needless to say, we didn't sleep much. I arose early and went outside to see how everything looked. I was surprised to find it a beautifully clear summer morning. The wind had shifted away from us, and you would never have known that disaster was just a few miles away. As I made my way back into the house, my cat, Roosevelt, dashed past me out the door. He never liked being cooped up inside, especially when the weather was so nice. He'd go off exploring for days at a time. I called for him but he just kept running. There was no way I could leave without all of us together and I prayed for him to come back. We waited, and about ten minutes later he came back and into the house on his own. It was another small miracle.

Nothing about the fire had improved during the night, so we decided to leave. The instructions were to tie a white sheet somewhere on the front of the house so officials would know the occupants were gone. The thought of leaving our home gave me a terrible sinking feeling in my stomach while tying that sheet. All we had was wrapped up right there in that house and that town.

We packed all we could in the RV and our two automobiles. The census included three dogs, three cats, one salamander, Jessie, Scott, me, and my favorite plant, a shamrock. As we pulled away I was thinking of all the things we were leaving. But, all of that we could replace or rebuild if we had to. Jessie was very upset leaving the only home she had ever known, making it a little harder to hold myself together for her. When I looked around me and realized that everything I really loved was right with me, I knew that whatever else happened would be okay. We had each other.

We headed out of town to the evacuation center to sign in. Our mountain had been declared an official disaster area, and signing in was the way the government accounted for displaced people. There were so many people there who seemed in shock and were just wandering about, not knowing where to go, or what they would do. We had our RV, so we could have gone to a campground somewhere. But most of the parks and camps in the area were closed, and those that were open were already full of evacuees. I had a talk with the angels and asked them to provide us with a place to park, some place pretty to comfort us and help us deal with our stress and grief. Maybe somewhere green, which was almost unheard of during that drought and, would it be too much to ask for some trees and a creek running by?

After we signed in, we drove out to try to find a place to stay. Thick, choking, smoke surrounded the whole area. In his truck, pulling the RV, Scott got a call from a friend in a nearby town which wasn't threatened, inviting us to park in his driveway. I was amazed when we pulled up to this friend's home. The spot he pointed out for us to park faced a huge green irrigated field on one side, and huge shade trees on the other! And, just a short walk away was a beautiful flowing creek! Thank you, angels.

That night I called upon the angels again to show me what was going to happen to our town and our home. I saw, with great clarity, all of us going home and our town untouched by fire. I was so relieved and decided to enjoy our time away as a vacation for our little family. We needed a break anyway, and our time together was a blessing.

Word came about a week later that it was safe to go home. We were one of the first back into town because we were able to stay so close by. The fire had made it right to the edge of town before being pushed back. Later, we would hear people speak of all of the prayers going out to save our towns and homes, and how people saw angels holding back the flames.

While discussing our experience when we got home, Scott asked how our thoughts had created our experience. I told him that I thought the fire was created by negativity and fear. Our experience, on the other hand, had been positive. We had been nestled all together, safely next to an irrigated field. And to round out that positive experience, our businesses, unlike so many others in town, jumped right back to normal levels as soon as we returned. So many people suffered that summer, many homes were lost, and some businesses never recovered. Our experience was positive for us because we were able to find happiness in being in the moment, detaching from the feeling of ownership of our "things," and allowing God and the angels to take care of the details.

I learned a lot that summer about myself and about happiness. It is not supposed to be complicated. As with everything else that is real and spiritual, it is quite simple. We didn't have any choice during that fire. It was going to happen anyway. We had to accept that we might lose our home and our businesses. We had to understand that we could not control any part of what that fire might change in our lives. We had to trust that we would be taken care of. Happiness is letting go of the worry and allowing the divine to take care of things.

Fourth Key: Love

We talked about "detaching" in the last chapter, letting go. And I am confident you spent some time learning to use that new Key. If you haven't, there's no time like the present to begin!

We started our journey with learning to believe that we can actually have the Kingdom of Heaven on Earth. We learned the meaning of that Kingdom is having in our lives, every day, all the wonderful qualities we associate with a heavenly existence, like, love, peace, joy, abundance, health, and happiness. These are the same qualities that a lot of people believe they can't get in this life, and it makes them want to check out whenever they feel that this planet is a little too intense for them. They think that the other side is the only place where they can get that heavenly existence. Most of us are looking for that Kingdom, and we can have it here. But first we have to believe that we can. When you say, "I believe that I can have the Kingdom in my life," you're literally telling God that you are willing to walk away from the stress, the anger, the fear, the strife. And you are willing to accept the Kingdom of Heaven on Earth in your life.

Next we learned about the Key of Trust. Once you believe that God can give you this love, peace, joy and abundance, your life begins to change. When your life starts shifting, particularly in a direction to which you're not accustomed, or in ways that you haven't counted on, you need to trust. Trusting means that you are depending upon something more powerful than what you see; something more powerful than you are.

Then, we moved on to the "Key of Detachment." Detaching is one of the harder Keys to learn, but one of the most important. We get attached to a particular outcome, or a particular idea of how things need to happen, or a particular way that someone needs to act. We feel our life should be going in a certain direction, or people in our life should be reacting to us in a specific way, and then we get all stressed because it doesn't happen the way we want it to. When you detach, you give up trying to tell God and the angels how to do it. They're really good at putting together what it is that you need, and they can do it better if you get out of the way and let them take care of the details.

Detachment means to live in the moment, to release your regrets about the past, and to let go of wringing your hands about the future. It also means to let go of anger, fear, jealousy; all the negative emotions.

How do you do that? Well, how do you quit smoking? You put the cigarette down. You don't light up again. How do you quit any habit? Worry, anger, jealousy, and winding yourself up into stressful circumstances are each habits of the way you react to life. It is really that simple and that hard.

When you find yourself getting into any of the negative emotions, like anger, fear, stress, etc., you must tell God, "I give this to you." That's how you begin reprogramming your reactions and freeing yourself of those addictions. You will have to remind yourself each time you begin to feel negative, and it may take telling yourself many times, until you can release it. You may find it helpful to call upon Archangel Michael to put himself between you and the emotion you are feeling, and to help you in the battle to give up those negative feelings to God. Continue to say, again and again, if necessary: "God, I am giving this to you... I'm giving this to you...I'm giving it to you."

No matter how many times you have to repeat this exercise, whether for minutes or days, you will end up giving that emotion and that situation, to God. Repeat this each time you are in the grip of anger or fear or worry. And eventually, when negativity starts to creep back in, you will find yourself thinking, "Oh, I already gave this to God, so I don't have to worry now, or be angry, or get stressed." Experts in behavior modification tell us that it takes twenty-eight days to break a habit or form a new one. It may be twenty-eight of the most important days of your life, because detachment is that important. If you are enmeshed in a negative emotion or situation, God can't talk to you, can't give you the signs, and you won't notice synchronicity. Also, the implementation of our next Key, the "Key of Love," depends upon that detachment.

Giving up a negative thought or feeling leaves us with space within our thoughts that we're not quite sure how to handle. We become restless because something is missing! We are so used to being filled with worry or anger that, once it is gone, we've got to do something with our thoughts. What has happened is we have created a void. In nature, a void cannot be tolerated. The universe will fill it with something. It will be filled by those feelings with which we are most familiar. This is where we need to begin using the Key of Love. Before we allow negative thoughts to reinsert themselves we must make a conscious effort to fill that void with love.

Instead of worrying about a situation you're in, or stressing about that person you love who's not acting the way you think they should, instead of stressing about all those things you were used to stressing about, you're going to put love into the situation. When you put love into any situation you are literally bringing God into it. God is love, and that love is unconditional. So the love you send in has no conditions. Conditional love is not love at all, but is nothing more than fear, and means that you are obsessing on the outcome. Let go of the outcome, get rid of the fear, and then bring in the incredible energy of unconditional love, which has the power to change anything that is going on in your life.

When you put love into a situation instead of the energy of worry, stress, or anger, it is like a giant sigh of relief. You can relax because you are allowing God into your life. You are wrapping the situation and your feelings in God's love. So now there is no longer a void. You let go of your negative emotion, detached from the outcome, and then you surrounded that person, that illness, the issue, with love. That's it. You're done.

It is that simple and very powerful. Still, I have people that come to me and say, "Linda, you don't understand... I'm dealing with a corporation, I'm dealing with someone who hates me, I'm dealing with my family, my job is at stake. You just don't understand." I say to them, "You don't understand." You don't understand that you are dealing with a divine energy that has the power to create and maintain this world, and can certainly take care of that petty little corporation you're contending with. You are dealing with the most powerful energy in the universe when you call upon love.

Let me tell you a very personal little story about the power of love to change lives. When Jessie was four years old, at the end of one school year, she made up her mind that she was going to go to school that autumn with her friends. There was one very big problem with that. To get into school a child needed to be five years old. She wouldn't turn five until seven days after the cutoff date. That summer, I heard about a testing program in our district for early entry, and had asked the principal of the school to put her name on the list. Shortly before the new school year was to begin, the school district changed their policy and had permanently discontinued that testing program, citing the high cost of administering the test and the low number of qualifying children. I made a few phone calls to the principal and members of the school board to ask them not to discontinue the program, but was told time and again that the decision was final. Finally, understanding that the issue was out of my hands, I put the whole thing into the hands of God, surrounded it with love and quite frankly, didn't give it another thought.

To let her down easy, I told Jessie what the principal had told me. But she continued to ask God to let her go to school, and was absolutely confident that she was going to ride that school bus with her friends. Nothing could dissuade her from that thought. A couple of weeks later, incessantly urged by my angels, I called the principal. He told me that he was about to call me to let me know that the school board had decided to test those kids who were on the original list. My assumption was that there were quite a few kids on the list, and perhaps those other parents had applied a little pressure to the school board too. Jessie was tested and accepted for kindergarten and was the happiest kid to get on a school bus that I had ever seen!

The amazing thing about this story is that out of that list of kids, Jessie was the only one tested that year. All of the other families opted not to have their children tested. No one else called about the testing, no one else wanted the testing. But Jessie got tested and Jessie went to school! The board of directors for the school district changed their minds somehow. A friend who worked for the school, told me that in the twenty-plus years she had worked there the school board had never reversed even one of its decisions. What's more, the program was discontinued after that. And testing for early entry has not been done since. But something made them change their decision that one time. And one very determined little girl got into school early.

The other amazing thing about this story is that such a powerful energy that can change the mind of a school board pays attention to the heart's desire of a little four year old girl. Is anything too small for God? No! Is anyone too small for God? No! The world was changed for Jessie in that moment. Even now, after all these years, I am still awed by what the power of belief, trust, detaching, and putting love into a situation can do. I am humbled by that, because I know there was nothing I did to make that happen for Jessie. She asked for it, I asked God to take care of it after I tried everything I could and failed. And God and the angels made it happen.

When you switch from engulfing an issue with worry to surrounding it with love, there is a huge change in the energy. Suddenly the situation takes on a whole different energy, which you can actually feel. In that moment change and healing begins. Nothing else can happen except healing when you bring in the energy of love.

So why are we running around in circles worried about things? Why aren't we simply bringing in the love, and letting God take care of things? It's not that we don't believe in God. Most of you are reading this book because you do believe in God. That is not ever the issue. What I find is that we just don't think that the energy of love, that divine energy, will actually manifest itself into our life. Either we don't feel worthy, or we just feel too small – a "God's got this whole universe to take care of" mindset. And then, there are the folks who think that only the people "doing God's work" will receive God's help. They don't understand that everybody is doing God's work. We each have our mission. Right now, yours is to have the Kingdom of Heaven in your hearts every single moment of every single day. Everything else that you do is just extra.

Think about this: If every single soul on this planet was conscious of their connection to God and that love energy, if they were detached, trusting, believing, and putting love into every single situation, the state of the world would be very different. There would be no hunger, no disease, no unhappiness, and the need for war would be eliminated. Are you a person that goes home and watches the news and worries about the wars in the Middle East? There are people who come to me distraught because they are so worried about the wars, the terrorism, and the feeling that the world is going to come to an end. What can make that change? How can you help? What have I been telling you throughout this book? You're going to believe, you're going to trust, you're going to detach, and you're going to put love into the situation. That means that you're going to send love over to the people in the war-torn areas; you're going to send love to the President, and the leaders on the other side. You're going to send love to the troops on both sides. Love is not political. It doesn't care about rank and distance is not a factor. Love is universal and works globally.

Worried about global warming? Send love. Surround the earth with love, because God is the energy of love, and any time you send love into any situation God is going to be there. God is going to be there taking care of the details, taking care of every little part, every little bit. You don't have to worry about or handle the details. Celebrate, because you don't have to come up with a solution to try to save the world. The solution is already there. You just have to invoke it. The more of us who do this, the stronger the energy created will be for change and healing. That energy can heal one person, whole countries of people, or the Earth. Nothing is more powerful than the energy of love, and when you bring that energy in, no evil, no discourse, no anger, no fear, can stand up against it. Nothing can stand up against the power of love.

When you follow these Keys, you will discover for yourself just how powerful the energy of love works. You will see that God didn't just dump you here on Earth without the means to succeed. God said to you that She loves you, just because you are here. What makes you special? You showed up for this journey on this planet. You are probably wondering, if this is true, then why isn't your life easier; why don't things happen for you? It's not working because you aren't following these Keys. It always comes down to you. God doesn't look down and decide who is deserving and who is not, who gets the good stuff and who gets the shaft, what makes one person joyful and another person not. There is no selection system out there. The whole concept of judgment is not true. God loves us all unconditionally, and indiscriminately. We are the only creatures that indulge in judgment. We are the ones condemning ourselves with that judgment! The God that sits on His big golden throne, trimming his long white beard, and deciding who's good and who's not, doesn't exist. That is the figment of some patriarch's imagination, designed to keep the "ignorant masses" in line. The masses are no longer unaware that myths like that don't make sense. The masses are no longer that gullible.

What is true is that God, the Energy of Love, gives us free will. Free will is the power of choice. Choice is a basic law of the universe. God gives us that choice because She loves us and wants our love in return, because we choose to love Her. Without the power of choice, there would be no reason for souls to exist, no reason for the universe, no Big Bang, no opportunities for enlightenment, no Christ, no Buddha, no Mohammad, no Earth, no nothing. Choice is there for the sole purpose of making our existence possible. How each of us succeeds in that existence is our individual choice. You choose to learn, or not. You choose to know God, or not. You choose to have the Kingdom in your life, or not. It is your choice to accept the gift of these Keys and to use them, or not.

Another law of the universe is that God won't come into your life against your will. You must invite the presence of God in your life. The purpose of these Eight Keys to the Kingdom is to show you ways to open yourself to God. When you choose to use these Keys, you choose to improve your life, to grow in enlightenment. When you use the Key of Love, you are putting God into a situation that troubles you and that situation starts to change immediately. That is another law of the universe. When you invite God into your life, it will not stay the same. The Energy of Love is purely positive. A life filled with Love cannot sustain negativity. We have been given the privilege to be here, to walk on this planet, to carry this love energy, to give it to others. I don't care how traumatic your issue is. If you're not bringing love in, if you're not calling it in to help fix your life, then you are making a huge mistake.

So you choose to let go and bring in love to surround your traumatic issue. Next, when dealing with the Divine Energy, you must stay in the moment. Don't be worried about tomorrow and don't be concerned about yesterday. When you're in the moment, and the love is flowing, you will receive instructions on what to do. How will you know? As I said before, God didn't dump you here without any communication abilities. You have been given that gift of intuition.

I know you were probably expecting an answer that would be simpler to understand. Maybe you were hoping for God to erect billboards outside your house that would tell you what you need to know for that day. But that's not going to happen. Or wouldn't it be great if God would just send us an email! That would be easy too, but it's not going to happen that way, either. Yet, intuitive communication is as simple as either of those. It comes from your heart center. You will "feel" the answers and instructions. How will you know it's from God? Because it's always about love! Always! When you ask, "How do I make this decision?" it's an answer that feels right for the situation, and is filled with love, so that it has a positive outcome for everyone involved. That doesn't mean there's no fear involved. But it feels right. Fear is a good thing to have occasionally, as long as it is not ruling your life. Fear helps us with our ability to analyze and decipher information, but sometimes fear makes us get stuck in our head and we analyze and decipher too much. Don't get stuck. Don't be afraid to make that journey from the brain to the heart, because you're working with love.

You will find that receiving the communication is not the hard part. The waiting is. And don't we hate waiting? You detach, you surround your situation with love, and then you wait. You're waiting for communication from God and the angels. You're waiting for the epiphany, the lightning bolt; that e-mail from God that says, "Okay, now do this." And we get so impatient. It's never fast enough for us. But while you're waiting, the synchronicity is being created on the other side. God and the angels are putting together exactly what you need. They are working to find the right people to fix your car, or to bring you comfort, or to make all the connections that are needed to get you the money you need. They are planning things behind the scenes.

Believe it or not, you do not have to control every detail. That's great! Enjoy that! Love is there to take care of every detail for you. And then when the waiting is over, you get a sign, you get a signal, you get a yearning. You know then that you are supposed to be doing something. God will lead you. It will be your turn, your action; an activity that needs to happen. It's all divine! "Let go, let God," we hear that all the time. Well, we're going to let go, we're going to detach, and we're going to bring love into the situation. And we're going to let God take care of all the details. There is no more for you to do but to follow your heart.

I know you are thinking that I make it sound so simple. But could it really be that simple? Yes, it is simple. You're in the now, you hear God's voice. You feel an emotion; you're led to do something. You follow through. And that's when miracles happen, every single day. There is no corporation, there is no lawyer, there is no policeman, there is nothing more powerful than God, and the energy of that Love. And when you embrace it and you call upon it, it will be there taking care of the details of every situation in your life.

This is not about just believing in love, not just loving God. It's about letting that love work in your life, letting that love work into your situation. Surround that corporation, that boss, that financial need, that ex-spouse, that in-law, with love.

I had a friend who was once in a courtroom situation: attorneys, judges, all of that. Being drawn into court can be incredibly stressful, because everything about it is dependent upon someone else's judgment. I suggested to her that before she went to bed at night, she should surround that judge, the opposing attorneys, even her own attorney with love, and then take love into the courtroom with her. In that same way you need to bring love into your situation.

Our usual reaction when someone is mean to us, or when we are embroiled in an issue, or when someone is not acting the way we want them to act, is to start complaining. "What the heck is the matter with them? Why can't they get things right? Why aren't they doing what they should?" For instance, my daughter woke up with a sore throat and all I could think about was, "If you would take your vitamins, if you would drink some more water, if you wouldn't eat fast foods, then your immune system wouldn't be so compromised." And she looked at me with tears in her eyes and said, "I'm really sick, Mom." Then I remembered. We need some love in here. So bring love. It's so easy to criticize. You want to break out of that habit. That's what detachment is all about. When we bring in and surround the situation with love, every negative thing melts from the power of that love.

My friend's courtroom situation came out just fine. In her words, "It was just amazing." Of course, it had to be, because there is nothing more powerful in the universe than God's love. You put love in, and all you've got to do is stand back and wait and let the miracles happen.

By the time we're done with these Eight Keys to the Kingdom your life is going to be so simple, and so easy, you are going to wonder what you ever worried about before, because God wants it to be simple, and easy, and abundant, and joyful. When things get out of whack, it's because we resist. We're resisting what's happening. We're resisting the direction our life is taking. We're resisting the flow of God in our life. That's what makes us a little crazy, what causes the stress and the depression, and taxes our bodies causing long term effects, even illness. Go with the flow. Believe, trust, detach, and then put love into that situation.

It really is that simple. It's supposed to be simple. It was never meant to be complicated, ever. We have complicated it with our own struggle. Don't resist anymore.

Meditation #4

As we start our meditation, Jesus shows up. He is standing before you because the ultimate sacrifice of love came with what He did. He is offering you the ultimate love situation, an opportunity to totally detach, to totally let go, and just fill your life, your heart with love.

And, my friends, if you don't think He was scared, think again.

He knows what it's like. So let's depend on that power of love in our lives. Let Jesus take the big heavy backpack filled with your troubles off of you, offering you the divine energy. Let that backpack go.

If there is a person for whom you are worried, surround that person with love now.

If there is a job situation, money situation, health situation that you're concerned about, surround it with love now. I always like to use the pink bubble as an example, because pink represents love. Surround that situation with a pink bubble and breathe love in to it. And then let it go.

Let that situation, surrounded by love, let it float away into the hands of Jesus, into the arms of God. He will handle it.

And now, in this breath, just this moment, thank God, because it's all taken care of now. Take a minute and just absorb that.

It's all taken care of...with Love

Linda's Story: Fear of Success

When Scott and I married, and built a home together everything was like a dream come true for me. I was respected and adored by my new husband, and I had a beautiful new home that was filled with love for the first time since my teen years with Nancy and Mom. You'd think I would have had the world by the tail. Actually it was quite to the contrary. I found myself incredibly depressed.

Yes, well, I didn't get it either. Day after day I found myself unable to cope and getting more depressed. I would start arguments with Scott for no reason. Things would get too peaceful and I would shake them up a bit. My insecurity made me crazy each time Scott was away for even a short while. He loved to go camping occasionally with his friends. And every time he would go I would freak out and think that he was leaving me, like my father and first husband had.

All of my worst fears kept creeping up into that wonderful, dreamlike relationship. Even as much as I had healed, I was still three-quarters of a tank low on self esteem. I had grown used to a life filled with turmoil and drama, and would be very scared when things got too calm and peaceful. When I would goad Scott into arguing, I would literally open the door and tell him, "Go ahead. You can leave now." He would laugh and look at me saying, "What are you talking about? I am not leaving. I love you." My certainty that all the men in my life would eventually leave me made me try to push them away defensively before they could make the decision on their own. It seems so silly now, all those irrational fears. The truth was that I didn't believe anyone could truly love me. I was sure they would eventually see that awful "real" me and realize their mistake. These thoughts were behind my insecurity with Scott because I had difficulties loving myself. How can you believe anyone else can love you when you're not even sure you know what loving yourself means?

On top of all this insecurity, the depression was getting worse. I felt so stupid. Why was I now getting so depressed after finally having some stability in my life? I couldn't figure it out then, but I understand it now. I finally felt safe. You'd think that would be a good thing, but I had never been safe before. There was no way I could lose my control in any of my previous relationships. I had to stay ahead of all that turmoil, protect myself; hide from the uncertainties. But being safe was different. It meant I could allow myself to actually start to feel. I had someone to really love me. All of the pent up emotions for all my life could no longer stay buried. I was finally safe to lose it, to let out the fear and anger, to go a little crazy.

Abuse survivors have incredible survival mechanisms. We bury the pain very, very, deep. So deep that we don't even remember. But the body was never meant to hold on to that much pain and emotion. God never meant for us to carry our burdens for twenty, thirty, forty years. That pain and buried hurt will eat away at the soul and then cause illness in the physical body.

When I work with clients, I explain it as like a jar inside us where we stuff all the negative emotion, and every time something happens to us we stuff in more and we keep a very tight lid on it. Eventually, we can't stuff anymore and we can't close the lid either. So we go to battle trying to keep all that emotion under that loose lid. When there is turmoil and stress in our life it is not just the immediate issue we are dealing with, but the unresolved issues from our whole life that have piled together.

Sometimes people just snap and have an emotional breakdown. They just can't keep the lid on the jar any longer. It started subtly for me, just some sadness, then a dread to end a nice weekend, then hating to get up in the morning. There seemed nothing to look forward to. In an attempt to overcome that seeming lack of enthusiasm, I spent a lot of time trying to add excitement to my life. I was constantly living in the future, making plans for something fun and exciting to be happy about; planning a tomorrow that would be better. Then when that exciting event arrived, I didn't enjoy it because I was still focused on the future, still planning more to look forward to.

Thanks to my obsession for shopping, I was always impeccably dressed in the latest styles and accessories, and never looked anything but cool and confident. No one knew I was really losing it inside. Deep in depression, I was my mother's child on that dark road that she had made all too familiar to me. Most of the time, I would space out, get lost in my head somewhere and not be fully conscious of where I was. I missed a lot that way. Other times I was immersed in negative feelings and thoughts, like when I would drive down our long road to town, thinking I would crash my car into a tree and, well, I probably wouldn't die. But I could go to the hospital and lie in bed for maybe six weeks. Here's the kicker: I thought everyone had thoughts like that.

Fortunately, I realized I needed help and I found a counselor. She helped me see many things more clearly, including that my crash fantasy was not a normal thought, and that healthy people don't think that way. While working with her, I experienced a moment of enlightenment, one of those moments that I now call a "universal aha!" It was like a light bulb going on, a profound truth for me. She said, "Just because your mother is not happy doesn't mean you can't be happy."

This was huge for me. I felt guilty whenever I was happy. I knew my mother was miserable and I never felt right if I was doing well and she wasn't. Many people do this same thing to themselves. Some of them attach these feelings to friends or relatives. Some attach them to the world situation, like, "Why do I have it so good when people are dying in Iraq?" Guilt is such a worthless emotion. At the base of it is fear. Fear that we don't really deserve good, fear it will be taken away. I was afraid that if I didn't worry enough about my mother, didn't give her proper attention and respect, that it would mean that I didn't love her enough.

Learning the source of my fear was the first time I began to know how far off of healthy I really was. It was also the first time I could see that there was a chance for me to be "normal," to feel like I fit into life, like I was not so different from the people around me. I may have had issues to deal with, but so did everybody else. I finally began to understand just how normal that is!

Saying Goodbye

That September day in 1990 when we adopted Jessica was the happiest day of my life, and the months immediately following were blissful. I wanted my mother to come out from Ohio to live with us so I could help her to have a happier life away from her abusive husband, in a home where she was truly loved and looked after. But she had already left her husband and moved in with her ailing mother to care for her. As much as she would have liked to come live with us, she was determined to stay and look after Grandma. But living with her mother was not a trip to the fair, either. My mother had leapt from the frying pan into the fire once again. Mom had always wanted to be a grandmother and I really wanted her to at least come out for a visit to meet Jessie. I called her again, just before Thanksgiving to urge her to come, but a visit was out of the question. Grandma would have no part of someone else caring for her, and insisted that her care came only from my mother.

All of her life, Mom craved love and appreciation from her mother, and it made her put aside all of her own needs to put her mother's needs first. She felt weak, and she hated that Grandma took advantage of that weakness, and then she felt guilty for hating Grandma. That guilt kept her obligated to her mother. Grandma kept control over my mother until the day she died. It's as if they made a very sick agreement to keep each other miserable. Less than a week after our Thanksgiving conversation, I got a call in the middle of the night. My mother had a massive heart attack and was taken to the hospital. No one was sure what would happen, but I knew she had already died. Her heart couldn't take the pain anymore and it just gave up.

My mother's death was the most horrific event in my life to that point. I was devastated in so many ways, not the least being that she would never be able to meet and know Jessica. While talking about this with a dear friend who had come to console me, my little three month old, sound asleep, started to giggle. My friend and I looked at each other in amazement, and he said. "I guess your mom has met the baby!"

There would be many times throughout the years that I would have signs of Mom's presence. But right then, I was too clouded with grief to sense it. Also, I had not yet learned that there would be other signs, or about my psychic abilities. Now, all these years later, after recognizing and honing my skills as a medium, which allow me to speak with many of the deceased, I understand the signs she was trying to send me. I understand that she was trying to assure me she was alright.

Arrangements had been made in Cleveland for my mother to be cremated, and a small memorial service was to be held afterward. The morning after we arrived in Ohio, I went to the mortuary to see her body one last time. I needed that closure. Incredibly upset, I was unsettled even more when I was lead into the large main chapel where she had been laid on a table under a sheet, naked and ready for disposal. I had not expected to see her that way. I had never before lost anyone close to me, had never even been to a funeral. I hadn't considered that clothes were not needed for cremation. I had expected that I might be shown into a private room, where I would probably see her through a curtain or screen. But there she was in that huge, empty, formal room, looking out of place as if she had been put there as an afterthought. It was all so matter-of-fact and impersonal. I stood there staring at her, scared and not knowing exactly what to do. I looked for the lines and wrinkles in her face that were so familiar, but they were almost all gone. It struck me how beautiful she looked, with almost a smile on her face of peaceful satisfaction. As I stared at her I began to feel her presence filling the whole room. She was there with me. It was real. I didn't understand how I could feel it, and I didn't know what to do with the feelings it invoked in me. It confused and frightened me. The only thing I could do was sob.

A few days later, we left after packing a few of Mom's things for shipment back home. She didn't have many possessions, but I found a few that were meaningful – just things – hoping to take something of her home with me. One of those things was a book she was reading, *The Shell Seekers*, a novel by Rosamunde Pilcher. As I read the book months later, I came across one line that I will always remember: "You never really grow up until your mother dies." I found particular truth in that quote. I was no one's little girl any more, and being grown up in that way made me feel very lonely.

Back at home as I was dividing her things, some to keep, and some to send to my sister, I was filled with an incredible, soul-deep sadness. That's when I smelled it, as if she had walked right past me. Her perfume! Channel No. 5, her favorite! Could I have imagined it?

Was there something near me that had her scent on it? I looked all around, I sniffed at everything, but it was gone. I thought it just my over-active imagination. But it seemed so real, as if she were there! After that, I had many dreams about Mom and would wake up feeling that I had been with her! Then I would realize it was just a dream. Contrary to what you might expect, this did not bring me comfort. It didn't matter to me that I was receiving messages from her. I was so filled with grief, that those messages brought little solace when all I wanted was to hug her one more time.

I had reached an emotional breaking point. Already stressed from years of trying to become pregnant, followed by the good stress – but stress, nonetheless – of adjusting to life with my new baby, my mother's death left me numb to everything around me, except Jessica. She was the one cord I clung to that kept me in reality. Looking back now, I don't know if Jessica came when she did because she knew Mom was leaving and I would need help, or if Mom felt it was safe to go because she knew Jessica was with me.

I knew what was happening to me, but I couldn't stop it. By Christmas I was starting to scare even myself, sinking into an awful depression. I became obsessed with the similarities between Mom and me. I could not get it out of my head that my mother had lived her life depressed, and I hated living that way. The only way I could see to honor my mother was to learn from her and refuse to be like her. I believe that was the point at which I began my journey to healing. Little did I know what lie ahead, what secrets would be revealed to me, or how hard it could be to face myself.

It took me five years after my mother died to reach a place where I was healed in regard to her passing. It was 4:30 A.M., December 1st. I always got up that early in those days. As I had become accustomed to doing, I thanked my mother for the life she had chosen, and congratulated her for having completed her purpose. I told her I missed her and understood that her going had also been her choice. That morning I was finally able to bless her crossing over. In that same moment a shooting star went across the sky. I knew Mom was letting me know she heard me.

The Angels Speak

Depression is such an insidious disease. Although I was determined to move forward in my life, the depression made me a physical and emotional wreck. I had been diagnosed with Chronic Fatigue Syndrome and slept all the time, but stayed tired. And my weakened immune system allowed me to stay sick most of the time with every cold or flu that came around. Then the depression began to reveal itself in another disguise. I started showing signs of compulsive-obsessive behavior. One way this behavior became obvious was in how I attempted to make myself feel better. I discovered that shopping and spending money lifted my spirits. But that high just wouldn't last, so I would have to spend more. Not actually having much money to spend didn't matter. But that's the problem with obsession, whether for alcohol, drugs, gambling, whatever. A compulsive-obsessive only thinks about their need to keep filling the hole.

I had a fear of the lack of money, which I learned from my parents' example. Whether or not money was actually tight, they were always overly concerned that they wouldn't have enough. The fear of not having enough stayed with me into adulthood and became broader in scope. Believe it or not, my fear of not having enough money led to my fear of not having enough food, enough clothes, enough shoes, enough...you name it! Shopping became my way of not only lifting my spirits for a while, but of fulfilling that need to have "enough." I figured out a way to shop without it costing me much of our limited money. I would go on a shopping spree and then take most of it back a few days later after the newness wore off. Despite the great temporary lift for my spirits, it was so hard handling the guilt afterward. I could not stop. I felt trapped in a wave of negative energy that kept lifting me up, only to dash me down again in remorse and continued depression.

You would never know by looking at me what I was going through. I was always well-dressed and looked like the picture of perfect health and confidence. My career in the business world was beginning to blossom. I was the only woman in the area managing an insurance office, and I was on the board of directors for the local Chamber of Commerce. Yet, back at home I would sink again, into the darkness.

I knew I needed to find someone to help me with more than just my depression, someone that could address all my health issues. But one of the drawbacks to living in a small town is a limited variety of services. Due to my feeling that conventional medicine had not served me well, I began searching for a local resource for alternative forms of healing but was not having much luck. One day my duties at the Chamber of Commerce brought me to the doors of a new business in town, to welcome them. To my surprise, the owner was a remarkable woman, courageous enough to offer her alternative health therapies in such a small community. I quickly signed up for acupressure treatments and found that they were just what I had been looking for, even though I didn't understand how they worked. These treatments were for balancing the energy in the meridians and clearing mental, emotional, physical, and spiritual blockages. It was my first experience with the concept of whole body healing.

With the help of this wonderful healer and teacher, I could feel my spirit come alive, as if I was emerging from deep inside. I felt myself becoming lighter emotionally, as well as physically. I found books to study on spirituality, angels, chakras, channeling, etc. I was learning how to release my anger and fear, and how to love and appreciate myself and life. It was then that I began learning to speak to the angels, and to listen. I made changes in my lifestyle for my physical health that included herbal cleansing to rid my system of the years of infertility drugs that had a negative affected my health. I would like to say that within weeks I was transformed into the confident woman I am today, but that's not so. It would take years, and in truth, I am still working on that transformation. The process of change never seems to cease. However, it does get easier.

Learning how God, the angels, and energy, works is one thing. Being able to bring it into our lives and make it work for us is totally another. We are creatures of habit. Even the habit of how we relate to changes, circumstances, other people, and life in general becomes deeply ingrained. In order for me to bring these new ideas into my life I had to change all of my old survival mechanisms. I can remember one morning as I headed to work, depression started to creep in again. I asked the angels what was going on, why I was getting depressed. Their answer was simple, "It's just a habit. Choose to be happy today. All is well." Messages and insight from the angels began coming to me gradually after I had spent hours, days, and sometimes weeks, releasing old hurts and angers, usually one at a time. I discovered that the angels had been talking to me all along. But I could not hear them, for all of my negative feelings were in the way.

As I worked diligently to take what I was learning and bring it into every aspect of my life, I found I was becoming very dissatisfied with my job. I began to see it as having no future for me, and thought that surely there must be more than working a nine-to-five job until I was sixty-five years old! All of a sudden it didn't make any sense to me. I questioned God, "Isn't there more to life? Shouldn't there be more?" Well, if you're going to ask, you have to prepare for an answer. The answer I got was that it was time to leave my job. But the very thought rocked my world. How could I leave? They needed me! What about my clients? What about that great income I was making? I truly felt there was no way I could leave.

Angels are so patient. I told no one about how I was feeling, but over the next three months business started to fall off the books. Clients I had for years took their business elsewhere. Feeling like I was backed into a corner, I gave in and told God that I would do what She wanted, but She would have to tell me what to do. The first thing I was told was to pay off my bills. As a chronic spender I had quite a few, but I worked diligently to make that happen.

In the meantime, I was still studying, meditating, and taking care of my health. But I felt I was not learning enough. That as great as it was, the knowledge I had acquired was inadequate. Once again, I was faced with living in a small town where it is hard to find what I needed, especially in the category of non-traditional spiritual studies. I asked God for someone to teach me more. About a month later, in the only metaphysical store in town, I met her. She was a wonderful Native American lady, a teacher, who did readings and worked with energy. We seemed to be drawn to each other, and she agreed to take me on as a student.

My new teacher had been living in Bisbee, a small town in southern Arizona, and was instructed by Spirit to put her house up for sale and move to property she owned in our mountains. She listened and put her house on the market. What she didn't realize was how much of a hurry the angels were to get her to our town. Her house sold in one week and she had only another week to move out. She had just arrived in town when we met in the store that day. I began studying with her a couple times a week for about three months. She told me she knew that Spirit's sending her to teach me must have been pretty special, because instead of having a usual group of five students for those three months, I was the only one.

After all the months studying, learning to work with the energy, I still didn't have a clue how God wanted me to use my new knowledge. I just knew I was very restless and the time was getting close for me to leave my job. By December of that year I had two very distinct messages, both dreams. In one I was told that my life was going to change drastically in the coming year. The other had me encountering a blonde woman who told me that she would be helping me to start my "healing work." In thinking about the dream later, it seemed that blond was familiar to me. But I had no distinct impression of what she looked like and couldn't remember how I knew her.

Even with these messages, I was starting to get frustrated, because I still didn't have a clear idea of what "healing work" I would be doing. One night, sitting in the yard with my husband staring at the stars, I saw what I took for a bright bolt of lightning that left a strange gold mark in front of me. As I stared at it I recognized, unbelievingly, that the mark was Sowelu, a symbol from the *Book of Runes* which stands for "wholeness." It was so clearly marked that I asked Scott if he saw it. Of course, he hadn't. It was just for me.

"Seeking after wholeness is the Spiritual Warrior's quest. And yet, what you are striving to become in actuality is what, by nature, you already are. Practice the art of doing without doing. Aim yourself truly and then maintain your aim without manipulative effort." – *Book of Runes*, by Ralph H. Blum

So many people think that there is such a thing as coincidence; that things just randomly happen with no rhyme or reason. There is nothing further from the truth. Most of us just don't take the time to see that these coincidences are ways that God is trying to tell us something. Signs are given to us all the time and we just choose to shrug them off. It would have been easy to write off my mother's shooting star as coincidence. The signs are everywhere. We can choose to question or doubt, but it seems like a waste of time to me. Just be grateful for the communication.

It was not long after the symbol of wholeness appeared to me in the night sky that I found myself "coincidentally" sitting across a table from the blonde woman from my dream.

Learning To Listen

It is amazing how hard the angels work to make our life everything we ask for it to be, and it is only in retrospect that we can see how truly dense we humans are. How much easier it could be if we would notice the work they do before we go through all the worry and stress that make us so sick, or so frightened.

I had been lead, pushed, and shoved by my angels to a point where I was just beginning to understand that there was a power in me that could make life meet all my expectations, good and bad. Lessons I learned because of my childhood, the loss of my mother, the struggle to find love, the feeling of powerlessness in getting a child, were finally finding a home inside me, making me anxious to continue learning more.

On the surface my life seemed to be heading in a positive direction. I had been led by the angels to teachers and healers that taught me how to deal with my depression and who put me on a spiritual path to wellness. I was also being led away from traditional means of employment, and had been told by the angels that I would be doing "healing work." But I was still in a phase of transition and it all still felt very incomplete.

So I waited for my life to change; waited for some clue to what healing work I would be lead into, blinded by impatience and an eagerness to know my future, so that I did not see the signs everywhere that change was already starting. It's times like that when you think that nothing is moving forward, like everything seems frozen in time or is moving in slow motion that we get so frustrated. We can't see it, but synchronicity is being prepared on the other side that will enable "coincidences" of events that will put us in the right place at the right time. Then when things do come together it seems to happen fast, because the groundwork has already been done on the other side.

When I think about all that time I was trying to get a baby, while I was suffering through the infertility treatments, somewhere in Idaho a seventeen year old girl was getting pregnant. The angels worked for months, maybe even years, creating the events that would bring that baby and us together. And when that plan was revealed to Scott and me, there were only three weeks to wait, three weeks to prepare to welcome our daughter. Yes, the angels weave a wonderful tapestry.

We can't see what they are doing. But if we can trust, they do a fabulous job of putting together all of our good into that weaving.

One afternoon I ran into my wonderful healer friend who first helped me through acupressure treatments a few years before. We hadn't seen each other in quite a while, so we made plans to have lunch the next week. During that lunch, she told me of needing a partner in her healing business and said she felt guided to me. I caught my breath as I realized she was the blonde lady from my dream! She offered to teach me everything she knew about being a healer, if I would become her business partner. Well! I couldn't wait to start! Finally things were moving on my side of the veil!

During those months of training, I felt like I was in my element. All of the work on learning how to get and stay healthy, clearing my anger and fears, and the years of study were coming together to fulfill my life's purpose. I prayed, meditated, met with the Masters on the other side while I slept. I knew this would be the work of my heart.

More clearing of my own issues was instructed by the angels. They didn't want me to be one of those therapists who hadn't healed their own lives before they offered help to others. And I agreed with them. I didn't want a client's issues to press my buttons. It seemed like a reasonable request, and I felt confident that I could do it. What I did not realize was what unbelievable memories would come out of the shadows of my repressed past.

We humans are such complex beings. We have such strength of will that we can hide memories of trauma within us so deeply that they seem never to have existed. I used to joke that I had no real memories of my childhood before the age of ten. My husband would say that that couldn't be a good thing. But I figured if I couldn't remember, that was for a good reason. Besides, therapy and all the acupressure treatments had cleared a tremendous amount, so I couldn't even imagine what more I could be holding on to.

I followed through with my meditations, and I made a request for the angels to guide me to the things I needed to clear. In these sessions I would imagine my angels surrounding me and leading me through a thick, cooling fog. On the other side of that fog I would view a scene sometimes from a past life, like being burned at the stake. But always the angels were there explaining how it related to this life. Sometimes I would come out of the fog to a place in my childhood.

There were reasons I knew these memories were real. First, each memory came with the emotions I felt at the time it happened, such as fear and humiliation. These emotions were very powerful. You see, it's not just the memories that are frozen inside of us, but the emotions of those moments as well. When unleashed, they all come flooding out. I actually felt four, or six, or eight-years old during these times. If the memories were going to be too painful when I came out of the fog, the angels would have me in a big movie theater. I would watch the memory come across the movie screen. It was a little easier that way.

The second reason I knew they were real, (as if feeling those emotions wasn't enough), was because it made sense with information or memories I already had. I also called my sister on several of these occasions and asked her what she remembered. She filled in many of the blanks for me. Some things that I didn't remember at all, she knew clearly.

Here's an example of my selective memory: Nancy, my sister, asked me, "Do you remember one afternoon when Mom got so mad she grabbed the potato chip bag and chips went flying everywhere?"

"Yes, I remember..."

"Do you remember her slamming the cupboard?"

"Yes, I remember that..."

"Do you remember spilling your milk?"

"Yes, I do..."

"Then, do you remember her smacking you across the face?"

No. I didn't remember that at all. And so it would go. We helped validate each other. I still use these techniques in my work today. I could tell you all the incidents of abuse that came up in those memories, but it would seem too unbelievable. If it hadn't happened to me I wouldn't believe it either. Let it be enough to understand that from a very early age I was a victim. The circumstances all around me just emphasized that position. This clearing took several months, and the techniques I learned for retrieving lost memories, validating and clearing them, were invaluable later in my healing work.

How does a little child become a victim? Well, that takes us back to my plan for this lifetime that I put together before I came here. I am very grateful to the angels for this clearing, and this book is to show my gratitude. But this book is not really about the abuse or about me being a victim. It is really about my plan and my journey from ignorance to insight, from hell to the angels.

Not all the memories and information were horrible. Some of it was just very informative. For instance, I wanted to know why I had to go through all the infertility stuff if the angels were just going to give me a child by adoption. So I asked them, and went into my meditation where again they took me through the fog.

When I exited, I saw the hospital scene when the doctors harvested my eggs during the in-vitro fertilization surgery. Nine eggs had been harvested, five were kept for me, and four were donated. The angels explained that the donated eggs created a child for a couple. The angels said I had karma with this couple from a past life and now it was fulfilled. I only saw the backs of the couple as they were walking away, but I saw the face of the baby. I was overwhelmed with a feeling of peace. The angels then made a promise that I would never have to go under the knife again. When I came to the end of the session, I felt such relief and was able to let go of my negative feelings about that whole time in my life. I was deeply grateful that something very good had come from all my pain.

Much more information began coming through; probably a good case for "be careful what you ask for." I asked to clear and by George, I was clearing. When my clients have unpleasant memories come forward, I tell them not to fight them or be afraid because they went through it once and survived. And they can do it again, this time for the last time. I have found that the hardest part isn't facing what happened, but trying to keep what happened from coming up and being released. The struggle, the part that makes us crazy, is trying to keep the lid on all that old pain. Once you remember and release it, the feeling of freedom is unbelievable.

When I was a child I was afraid of the dark, even with a nightlight on. I was afraid of who or what might be in the closet or under the bed. Even into my thirties, waking in the middle of the night gave me the willies. Think of it, still scared of the dark even as an adult! When the memory came to me of my father sneaking into the bedroom at night, I realized it wasn't the Boogie Man, but just an ordinary man and I had nothing to fear. I remember thinking to myself, it's just him. I have been afraid all these years, and it was just him. I wasn't even surprised or angry at my father. I was just relieved that the fear was gone. I am not afraid of the dark or waking up in the night anymore. When I awaken now all I can feel is the love of the angels and too, I always remember how scared I used to be and this flood of relief comes over me again.

I worked at this cleansing for months, clearing what I could and remembering what the angels thought was important for me to know.

When the time came to leave my job at the insurance office I was ready. My husband was very supportive and excited for me. When I first told him I wanted to leave my job to do this healing work, his only comment was, "Must be nice to know what you want to do." Yes, it certainly was. Finally.

I would get little validations to let me know this change in my life was right. For instance, while standing in line at the grocery store I saw an ad in a magazine. A man was about to step off a cliff and a hand was reaching up to carry him to the other side. I felt like the man in that ad. I knew I was being carried, but by a flow of energy. It could not have been easier for me to make the transition from employee to independent business person, from being healed to giving healing. Clients started coming to see me right away. All the signs pointed to the time being perfect; the type of healing practice was the right one, and I was the right person to do it. It was really easy! It's supposed to be easy. And I never want to forget that! If I had let fear creep in, I would have been miserable and I would not have followed the angels' urging to make that big change.

It was shortly after going into business that I became president of the Chamber of Commerce. While I had been treasurer, I had noticed some things in the finances that didn't seem quite right to me. I had brought the issue to the attention of the then president, who chose to look away. As president, I looked into the situation to find a huge problem that included fraud. I began the battle to try to get the board to understand that the situation needed to be addressed, and that sweeping changes were needed to prevent a similar occurrence. The members did not all agree to the seriousness of the situation, and resistance was very strong to making a correction. The interesting part of this story is not the details of what happened and why, but that I knew I was supposed to be there during the most stressful period, handling the most important issues that the Chamber had ever had in its history. I was there to push the changes forward, to participate in the most stressful meetings, and to butt heads with the most stubborn people. Fortunately, I knew angelic help was always near.

One specific meeting comes to mind, for which I was particularly worried, knowing it had the potential to explode. Before I went in, I called upon my angels and the angels of everyone else attending, to be at the meeting with us for the best and highest good. The meeting progressed well and by the end, personalities that had clashed vehemently in the past were laughing together and giving each other "Atta-boys." I was totally amazed at how well the angels did their work.

Driving home after the last meeting at the end of my presidential tenure, I looked at the potted plant I received as an appreciation gift, thinking how anti-climatic it all was: a potted plant for two years and hundreds of volunteered hours of my time. I wondered why I had even done it. There was no big recognition for me, no hoopla, no balloons and streamers, and very few "thank yous" from my fellow board members. The angels so clearly said, "You weren't there for the recognition. You were there because God wanted you there."

Yes, God does care about a little Chamber of Commerce in a little town in the mountains of Arizona. I knew the angels were right. I wasn't supposed to get noticed. I was just supposed to do what needed to be done. And the angels made it easier.

The Business of Angels

As I write and recount circumstances that have shaped my life, I am amazed at how incredibly God and the angels work. There was never a moment in my life that I wasn't in divine energy, but there were times when I chose not to pay attention. That was not deliberate though, just my own ignorance. I have learned since, that sometimes ignoring what's going on is a good thing because the less I stress, the more efficiently the angels can work. That sounds simple, and when I stay out of the mix it is simple.

We humans have such a hard time with simplicity. We always want to over analyze things. There's too much work going on in the mental plane. Personally, I don't want to do that much mental work, especially on issues that the angels handle better than I do anyway. For example, when my husband asked me how many clients I needed to see each week in order to pay the business's bills, I told him I didn't know and that the angels would take care of it. That works for me. I know that not everyone can go through life that way. But if you can grasp some of the concept, it will make your life easier. If I had tried to figure out how many clients I needed to see, I would have made myself crazy waiting for that number of people to show up. So I let God become my day-planner, because for me sometimes ignorance is just bliss.

My new business took off from the "git-go." My appointment book was filling up and I was doing what I loved. After a couple of months, my insurance sales license renewal came in the mail. I was undecided what to do, renew or discard it, hesitant to narrow my options. I had thirty days to decide. But shortly thereafter, business started slowing down. People weren't coming. I was perplexed. Wasn't I doing what the angels asked? That was when I was shown in a very dramatic way that our thoughts create our reality. My reality had become about fear of failing, and the lack of clients was reflecting that fear. There is no "fence sitting" when working with the Divine Energy. It's an all or nothing deal. It wasn't that keeping my license was such a bad thing, but the reason behind why I wanted to keep it that was screwy. When you make a commitment to follow your heart, which is always connected to the divine, the whole universe supports what you do. That's all the backup you need. I took the renewal and threw it away. As far as I was concerned there was no turning back. Once that was done, my appointment book was full again and

I haven't looked back since. The next year, when the second renewal came in the mail, I didn't even think twice. I just threw it away.

It takes a lot of faith to totally uproot yourself and follow your heart. I see it with clients all the time. The angels speak to their heart and they want to move forward. But the fear can be all-consuming. In all the years of operating a business, I have had to override my fears more times than I can count every time business slowed down. I truly understand how frightening it can be. What needs to be understood is that our fear, our belief that God will not meet our needs, will keep our good from coming to us. As I look back on all the preparation and validation that the angels gave me, it is quite obvious that I am where I was intended to be. That same energy that validated me every step of the way is the same energy that supplies all my needs year after year. It really is that simple.

My first business opportunity was a partnership, and partnerships are funny things. As my end of the business got stronger, hers started to flag. My clients were coming, hers weren't. As my partner began to allow fear to creep in, her business got worse. She began taking chances and making decisions that she would not have made except out of fear. When fear sets in and we act out of desperation, circumstances backfire against us. Her decisions were costly, which I then had to make up for. Unfortunately, I could not make up for all the losses, and we accumulated quite a debt, some of which I was responsible for. I had a lot of respect for her and still do. But inevitably, the time came to end our partnership.

Ending a business partnership is a little like a divorce. We had to find a way to divide the assets. When I went to the angels for guidance, they told me to accept whatever offer she made me. It wasn't long after that she came to me with her offer and I accepted it, debts and all. It didn't seem quite fair to me, but the angels had told me to take whatever she offered, that it would all come back to me. Over the years that has proven to be true, and I have been blessed because of the time she and I spent together. I bless her for her help in getting me started in my own practice and for her part in my healing and growth.

Once again, I felt like the angels had asked me to step off a cliff and have the faith to be carried to the other side. Talk about fear! I was now doing alone what had taken two of us to do: a secretary, supplies, rent, utilities; the whole show. My old fear of the lack of money rushed in again. I would be haunted by that for years, and it still creeps up occasionally. Now I just look back and use my 20/20 hindsight to see how God has taken care of my every need.

Through all of this, the most important message I received was to focus on the quality of the work and the angels would take care of the quantity. I knew if I didn't have the purest of intent, my business would be shut down. I saw it happen to my partner when her concerns about the business made her turn her attention away from her purpose. The angels don't mess around. They instruct me on every aspect of the business, from what care is needed for an individual, to how much to charge. I am grateful for the love and guidance that has been given me.

This love and guidance is not exclusive. It is for all of us. I am sure that some of you, reading this now, may think that this guidance only comes to a few, those with a special mission. Well, each one of us is special, and we all have a mission. Some missions are wide reaching and take a lifetime commitment. Others may be just to smile each day at our co-workers, or add some light to someone's day while serving breakfast at a drive-thru, all the while dealing with issues that keep us stressed, or out of money, or out of good will. Each of us has our own purpose for being here. Not all of us need to be a Mother Teresa in order to fulfill our purpose and get guidance. Our truest mission is to recognize our true selves, and to remember that when we take the steps to honor ourselves, the whole Universe supports our efforts with synchronicity, doors open for us, and help and guidance is always there for the taking.

One evening, I was thinking about where I was in my life. It seemed like I had reached a certain plateau. I had always felt that my life had been an uphill climb and I realized that things had become easier. I felt like I had reached the top of the mountain! And, wonder of wonders, I was thinking how far I had come, instead of how far I had yet to go! Everything I asked for I had received. I had wanted a home of my own, a wonderful husband, a child, and a job I loved. I had it all, and I was sitting right in the middle of it. I was flushed with appreciation for all that good. What a weird feeling that was, to feel like a victor instead of a victim. With the help of Heaven I discovered my path, my talent, my heart's desire, my purpose, and had accomplished all I had been guided to do. I didn't know what to expect next. I had always been so busy climbing that mountain, striving for something, pushing and prodding to move forward. I had become accustomed to needing something to obsess about. As I sat there wondering what to do next, the oh-so-familiar voice of the angels said to me, "Now just enjoy your life."

I sat back with the deepest feeling of contentment and promised myself that I would learn how to do that.

Fifth Key: Humility

We have come halfway in our journey to acquiring the Kingdom of Heaven on Earth in our daily lives. The first four Keys, Believe, Trust, Detach, and Love, are substantive tools, rules of the universe, without which the essence of that Kingdom cannot be accessed. The next three Keys are attitudinal in nature, and once we allow the Kingdom to come into our perception, these Keys are qualities that will allow us to better understand the nature of the Kingdom, and help us prepare ourselves to receive the benefits it offers.

Now that we have chosen to own the first four Keys, we Believe we can have the Kingdom; we Trust that God and the angels will take care of everything, we have Detached from our expectations of where, and what form our best and highest good will take, and we rely upon our infusion of Love to neutralize all negatives in our lives.

Key five, "Humility," was not so easy for me to understand at first. So I went back to the angels. I am very sensitive about giving the wrong impression about what kind of humility is required of us, since it is the first Key that asks us to alter our attitude and is not to be used alone, but rather in combination with each of the other Keys. Over the subsequent two weeks, the angels gave me many signs and examples that showed me what they wanted.

Let's define "humility" so we can put it into the context in which the angels want us to use it. First, we want to understand what the Key of Humility is not. It is not being inferior, insignificant, or subservient. It is not expected that you demean yourself in any way. These definitions can have negative aspects to them, and are not at all the meanings intended for this Key. God and the angels want the purpose of these Keys to be about your empowerment. By accessing their energy, you bring that empowerment to you. These Keys give you the tools you need to use that empowerment to improve your life and your connection to God and the angels. My purpose for speaking about angels, and for bring them to people's attention, is to help people grasp their empowerment and put it to work for themselves.

When we speak of empowerment, power, it's not the kind of "worldly" power that most people think of, like the power of people "in power," such as presidents, kings, dictators, etc. That kind of power is about control. It's about power over people, over things, and over laws. We perceive people in high positions or with a lot of money, as having power. With enough money, you can own a corporation; you can make rules that other people have to follow; and you can make people feel financially vulnerable. But that kind of power has a negative side because as long as you have control, you have the power. Once you lose control, your power is gone. Worldly power is about the fear of either losing your power, or someone else gaining power over you. People all over the world are fighting and killing each other in a tug of war over this kind of power.

When we talk about being humble, I do not mean that it's the opposite of having power. We are also not suggesting that anyone become a doormat. There are already too many people who don't really love themselves, who allow themselves to stand in the background, working hard but unwilling to take credit, because they either think of themselves as unworthy, or believe that to be righteous they must be this kind of humble. In the meantime, all the energy and enthusiasm for life just gets sucked out of them. When you truly love yourself, you don't allow yourself to be put in that position. So don't confuse being a doormat with the humility that the angels want you to have.

God wants you to understand that true humility – being humble – is not an attitude that can be affected by worldly power. The empowerment you receive from God and the angels is a spiritual power, which is not about controlling. We don't need to control anybody or anything, which is one of the lessons we covered in the chapter on Detachment. Real spiritual power is not a struggle. In fact, it's very relaxing. It's a knowing. It's a believing. It's a trust. It's a detachment. It is love.

So what is it that we're talking about, then, when we say, "be humble," or "have humility?" It's the other definitions for those words: courteously respectful; not proud or arrogant; the modest sense of one's importance and power. Most of us have felt this feeling of smallness – humility – in the face of some tremendous natural wonder, like the power of hurricanes, the grandness of the Grand Canyon, the vastness of space. Who cannot look up into the star-filled night sky and not be humbled by the presence of God in its creation? What the angels want you to feel is that same humility when you stand back and look at what God has done in your life. It's about seeing what that divine presence has accomplished, so you can be aware as it is continuing to work in your life.

Let's look at the power of God as we have experienced it in our lives. Take just a moment and pick something out in your life. Your first thoughts may be about the big, important, easy to see, blessings you have been given. Speaking for myself, I first see the miracle of my child and the great person that I married. Perhaps you have been blessed in that large way. Feel humble before the power of God that brought those blessings to you. Some of you may have to look really hard to find anything. It is you the angels are especially addressing. They want you to see even what you think is insignificant, and know that it was God at work in your life. Look at that small thing, that something that made your life different, better. Maybe it was quitting smoking, or that you found something wrong with your car and fixed it before it blew up and cost you a month's wages to have repaired. Maybe it was meeting someone who became your best friend, who in turn gave you a puppy that now brings great joy to your life. If something that small changed your life, it had great power. And God is in that power. Let that great power awe you and humble you. In my life I don't have to look far to find something overwhelmingly humbling to me. Just having the angels come up with the Eight Keys to the Kingdom and the energy it has taken on; how far this little message from God has traveled is very humbling. Look at the power of God and what it can do in your life. It has even brought this message to you.

So when we talk about humility and about being humble, it is to know that something besides you, something besides our president, something besides your boss, something besides your relatives, is really in charge of your life. That something is the Energy of Spirit, God, the angels. And it is available to each of us. We don't have to do anything special to earn it. Now that's humbling!

Being humble is having a kind of self confidence where you don't have to take yourself too seriously. You can laugh at yourself for making silly mistakes, and admit to making important mistakes without wasting time beating yourself up, which then allows you to immediately focus on correcting the mistakes or admitting that you can't fix them. Humility needs to be brought in because it keeps you grounded, and allows you to admit that maybe you don't have all the answers. Maybe you don't know what to do about your situation. Maybe you're not the one to make that decision.

Humility will keep you in a place of allowing God to come in and do the work that needs to be done in the most efficient, loving, blissful manner. This is the humility we are talking about. This is the humbleness that we want you to understand. There is a power out there that has more knowledge, more wisdom than you could ever hope to have in your lifetime. And it is weaving this incredible tapestry in the background for your life. Giving up the control, allowing you to say, "Maybe I don't know everything. Maybe I'm not the one to solve this," is the humility we want you to engage.

Engage humility – and listen to this very carefully – even if, and especially if you are the strongest person you know. If you are the "go to" person in your family, in your company, in everyone else's life; if you are the person who gets all the difficult situations dumped in your lap, believe it or not, there are issues that you cannot, and even should not solve. But you are strong and feel that you must, because all those people who are not as strong as you are counting on it. You strong people have the hardest time giving up, letting go, and letting God take care of it. And this is what "being humble" is all about. It's not about diminishing you. It's about lifting you up by knowing that you are a part of some incredible energy that keeps the planets in place. This love energy, that we call God, flows through you. And that is humbling.

My friends, there are always going to be things in your life you have no control over. Get used to it. It's okay to not handle it, to say no, or to admit you can't. Let it go! Struggling against it will only make you stressed and unhappy. I see it all the time in my practice. People franticly crying, "I can't control this! I can't control this!" You're not supposed to. That's the ego telling you to "handle this, take care of this, you're better than this, take control, you should know more, you should do more!" Nonsense! Why do you do that to yourself, put such pressure on yourself to resolve issues you have no business attempting? It's not always up to you! You don't always have the answers! But you continue to whip yourself by believing it is up to you. Then what happens when you can't figure it out? The ego starts in on you, telling you that you're "worthless, you failed, you should have known better, you should have tried harder." That's about the time that people come to see me in my practice. They have been devastated by their failures. They've been trying to change a person, a place, or a thing, or even the world, and they haven't been able to succeed. They're having trouble with themselves, feeling guilty because they couldn't fix it.

I know there are people out there that are feeling that same thing. I want you to look at this and see the truth of it, because it is your ego that keeps you pounding your head against a brick wall. And after a while that pounding just gives you a headache. You know, it's not the brick wall giving you the headache. It's your relentless need to pound against it. Give it up. Let it go! It's not only okay to admit that you can't break down the wall, it's what the angels want you to do. Be humble enough to ask them to breach the wall for you. Be humble enough to trust them to take care of it. Use humility to effectively detach, knowing they can do it better than you. And then surround that wall with the simple, humble, uncomplicated love that has no conditions. You have to have humility in each of the first four Keys, and once you do, it will expand the effects of each one, because humility forces you to be submissive to that power outside yourself and say, "I don't know what to do. You take care of it, God. I'm done."

I am humbled by that power that will step in and take off and fix, change, and maneuver things to work for the best and highest good of everyone involved. You hear that? Not just you. Everyone involved. I am humbled by that power! Therefore, I allow that power to work in my life. That's how humility works. From that place, where you step back and say, "I can't fix this, I can't change this person, I can't change the world," you then have the ability to say, "I am giving it to you God. I humbly submit. It is yours."

And from there, in that moment of letting go, my friend, you are empowered.

Here is a little story about empowerment that hopefully will demonstrate how the use of these Keys, coupled with Humility, can make the world a little different:

Scott and I had promised our daughter for her sixteenth birthday to pay half the cost of her first vehicle. Being the metaphysics teacher that I am, I brought her up to set challenging goals and then manifest and create their fulfillment in her life. In short, I taught her not to settle. By the time her birthday arrived, she had saved her half of the cost so Scott took her out to the local car lots. But everything she liked was way out of the price range. It was obvious that we had greatly underestimated the expense, so we upped our portion of the budget.

The following weekend, with our new budget firmly in our minds and Jessie's dream firmly in hers, we visited every dealership on the mountain. And we found nothing satisfactory. I continued to encourage her to keep creating and manifesting what it was she wanted. At the same time, I was manifesting that we were going to find something within our budget and it was going to be simple and quick. Frankly, I kept finding little old clunkers and tried to seduce Jessie into wanting one. "Oh, Jessie! Look! Here's one that's cheap, AND you can drive it home today!" But Jessie found something wrong with each one. Wrong color, wrong size, wrong brand; just not what she wanted. She had her heart set on a pickup, and not just some old something from somebody's farm. I was biting my lip, because I'd taught her not to settle and everything in me was begging, "Jessie, I'm tired. Just settle!" We found absolutely nothing that put a light in her eyes.

We planned a trip to Phoenix the following Sunday to see what we could find in the vast selection there. We began our search with a private owner then moved on to a number of dealerships, but found nothing interesting or within our budget. Jessie was getting a little discouraged, and her parents' patience was getting thin. We decided that we would try one last place before starting back up the mountain. The dealership we pulled into had all their trucks marked above $18,000 – way too much! I didn't even want to get out of the car, but Scott encouraged me to "just take a look." Not expecting to find anything in our price range, we got out and scanned the lot. Lo and behold, there it was! My daughter got out, took one look, and her eyes popped. She had found her first love!

It was shiny black, with blue flames running down each side, every bell and whistle you could ever want, including a six inch lift that made it difficult for Jessie to haul her butt up into the seat. It was a guy magnet and she was thrilled! I was sure we would have to break her heart because the price on it was pretty high. I pulled the salesman aside and told him I would take it for not a penny more than $7,000 less than the sticker price. I was thinking it was probably not going to happen so I told Jessie, "We don't have time to deal. If this doesn't work we gotta go." My daughter was behind me working on manifesting that truck into her life like crazy. The salesman came back with his head down and said, "I'm really sorry. The best I could do is $500 more than you want to pay." Is that all? We took it for a ride and within twenty minutes the deal was sealed. We were out the door and on our way home.

There is more to this story than just two indulgent parents trying to make their only child happy. The dealership was not usually open on Sundays. They opened for just a half of that day, from 11 A.M. to 4 P.M. because business had been a little slow the previous month. We showed up at 11:30 on the only Sunday they were open in the history of their dealership. The salesman told us that four other people from the day before were considering the truck, and another interested couple had been in just before us. Scott looked it over very well for mechanical problems and found none, (we discovered how mechanically reliable it was in the months that followed, so we know that it had no major defect). There was no reason for them to discount the price as much as they did. I looked at my daughter as we drove out of the lot, and asked her in total wonderment, "How did you do that?" You know what she said to me?

"Jealous, Mom?"

Jealous? No. But as I rode home with her, watching her drive that hot, fabulous truck, and thinking about what a great deal it was, I was totally awed. It made me think about this Key. And I was humbled at the power that this child was able to embrace and make work in her life. I was humbled before the power of God that prompted a dealership to break its tradition and open on Sunday, and humbled by that same power which allowed no one else to claim that vehicle before we found it. Jessie created all of that, drew that power to her, without even a blink of an eye.

Yes, in the large scheme of things, that truck may have been a pretty small objective in the dream of a fairly average teenage girl. But it was the power of God that made it happen. And the example it shows us is that we can all embrace that power! That truck came to Jessie because she put her faith in that power. It's the same power of God you can harness to make changes in your life, and if it can make dreams that are only important to a young girl come true, think what it might do for the important things in your life! I am humbled by that power because it makes even small dreams come true. I am awed and I submit to that power! I know that power is all good. My daughter obviously knew it. She got exactly what she wanted, and even at age sixteen, knew she did not have to settle.

Although I'm pretty proud of myself for not forcing my daughter to get a truck she didn't want, in the end, I had nothing to do with her dream coming to her. She held on. She never doubted that she would get the one she wanted. She didn't push, or whine, or wheedle. She just waited for the "power" to bring her to that truck. Right place, right time, right truck and the right price and – "voila!" Dream come true!

There is not a problem, a relative, a friend, a boss, an issue about money, or health, or happiness that can stop God! Humility is submitting to that power, giving in and letting that power do what it does best. Where you feel you have to knock down doors, the power of God simply turns hearts around so that the doors are opened for you. Humility, admitting that your efforts are not the only way to get things done, is the Key that Power uses to open those doors.

Humility is also an understanding that you're not supposed to do anything unless you're told. Step back, turn it over to God. "I'm humbled, God. I give it to you. I don't have the answer to this. It's yours." And then wait and listen. When that answer or those instructions come to you, humility is about acting when you need to act. You give it over to God and then you receive your empowerment. When you get into doing this, it's as though you have no problems. God's taking care of everything for you!

Sometimes we find ourselves enmeshed in a situation of emotions, or that's full of chaos, and it fills us with confusion and disappointment, and makes us wonder, "Why? What's going here?" Humility is about realizing that it is not always about you, that most of the time, your life is really about all the other people in it. Maybe your involvement is just like what my involvement in the Chamber of Commerce was. I was there because God needed to make some changes in the life of that group. Maybe you're involved in your issue to change some energy. Maybe you're there to make an impression in someone's life. Maybe, just maybe, that temporary situation has nothing to do with you at all. Let the situation be taken care of by God, because the more love you put in, and the more trusting you do, and the more you believe, the more quickly the situation will be over, than if you just whine your way through it.

The Chamber of Commerce would have been bankrupt if the financial bleeding had not been discovered and stopped. The negative ramifications would have been felt throughout that town and the others around it for years to come. I had nothing to do with the problem, but I was thrust into the middle of it all. Now, maybe the situation would have been resolved even if I had not been there.

God would have just used someone else, I am sure. But I believe with all my heart, that I was supposed to be the one heading up that group at that crucial time because there was a huge lesson in it for me, too. For a short time after the dust settled, I was disappointed that the other board members had not shown their appreciation in the way I had expected. The angels were quick to make it very clear that I was not there for that kind of reward. Although I had expected differently, it absolutely was not about me.

Does God care about all of that? Yes! And that makes me feel humble and as tiny as standing in awe under that magnificent night sky, that the greatest power in the universe, God Herself, got involved in that little group of people. That She came to rescue that little town in the mountains from fraud and bankruptcy. I am just as humbled that She has shown Her love for Jessie in so many ways, like getting her into school a year early and seeing to it that she got her great truck. Each of these interventions changed the world for every person involved. Some seemingly small changes may prove to have the largest rippled effect – a young girl learning at a very early age to believe and trust in the power of God. Who knows where that could lead? The largest issue, which on the surface might have had the widest range and most dramatic outcome, may have been just to show one emerging psychic medium that the world was much bigger than she thought it was at the time, and that she was much smaller.

God is that powerful! In the face of love, that awesome humility requires us to offer our service to it, to submit ourselves to say, "How may I be of service to you, God? How may I serve?" One way to humbly submit to that service is to say, "I understand that it may not be about me, and I am okay with that."

Florence Scovel-Shinn, who gives us our affirmation for this Key of Humility, puts it this way:

"All power is given to me to be meek and lowly of heart."

What does that mean? I don't like anything that even hints of being a doormat, so let's think about it. It takes a lot of strength to say "I don't know...I can't do it." It takes strength of character, strength of spirit, strength of faith, and the biggest one, strength to overcome our pride, our ego, to achieve true humility. This affirmation is telling us that we are given the power, the strength, to do whatever it takes, including stepping back and giving God the lead. "All power is given to me to..." step back from this situation. "Meek and lowly of heart..."

Say, "I don't have the answer here, God." You have the power within you to be able to do that, and to give yourself permission to say, "I'm okay with that."

Florence's affirmation continues on to say: "I am willing to come last, therefore I am first."

You don't have to puff yourself up to anybody. Humility is about being real, not adding to your own self worth by aggrandizing your contribution. It is necessary to be unpretentious and unaffected by what you imagine to be your role in the successes of your life. You have heard the saying, "Hard work is its own reward?" No it isn't, unless you love hard work. The reward is in knowing that you didn't have to do it by yourself, in knowing that God loves you so much that She was right there the whole time making sure everything was working out for you. I worked very hard for two years to help that Chamber solve its problems. But others worked just as hard in their own fashion and listening, as they would, to their own angels. The intent of that group changed, over time, from intense self-interest to one of magnanimity. I am overwhelmed and awed by the angels' accomplishment in bringing people so doggedly opposite together for the best and highest good of that Chamber and that community. Today the Chamber is not only alive and well, but very strong and well respected, thanks to the angels.

If you're doing what you do from your heart, being led by God, you don't have to impress anybody, because the energy of your purpose and your actions will speak for themselves. I meet a lot of people and I never tell them what I do unless they ask. If they ask, I will tell them. If God wants us to strike up a conversation about what I do, it will be expanded upon. Otherwise, they will go, "Oh, that's nice." And we move on to talk of other things. You don't have to tell anybody how great you are, or how spiritual you are, or about anything you are accomplishing, because the energy is there. And while you're so busy spouting off how incredible you are, you are missing whatever it is in the moment that God wants you to get.

"I am willing to come last, therefore I am first."

I am willing to step aside and say, "God, I give my trouble to you to handle because you can do it so much better." Personally, I don't know why you wouldn't want to hand it over to God. If somebody, even me, came to you and said, "Let me take all your cares and worries and I'll handle them all for you," wouldn't that give you a rush of relief? Well, somebody better than me is offering you that deal. God is offering. Let it go! Be humbled by the power and the strength that you are working with. And that power and strength will work through you.

And when it's time for you to do something, you will know when and what you are supposed to do. You will know if you are supposed to talk to somebody. You will know if you are supposed to be at....McDowell and 24th Street on Sunday afternoon at noon to find the best truck on the planet. You will be compelled to work your hardest for a purpose you feel strongly about. You will know! You won't miss anything. You can't, because when you step back and allow yourself to be humbled by that power you immediately are in the present moment. And when you are in present moment, God can then communicate with you. And all of your believing, and your trusting, and detaching, and your love, will come together. And, my friends, that's when your life becomes simple and easy. Who doesn't want that?

Meditation #5

Allow yourself to invite the power of God to come to you. Step back from whatever issues you have going on, whatever troubles you may think you have, and pile them at the feet of this power.

For just this moment, understand the power that you are allowing in to your life. Allow yourself to know that the most powerful energy in the universe is now standing in front of you.

Let the impact of the importance of this moment fill you with awe that this most powerful energy has come to you, for the sole reason that She loves you. Let yourself be filled with humility that She comes even to you and offers to make Her power work in your life.

Submit yourself to this power. Invite Her to take the pile of troubles you have laid at Her feet. Let them all go. Say goodbye to those troubles with a knowing smile that they will all be resolved by the experts.

All you have to do is say "yes" and let it go. The prize, my friends, is the Kingdom of Heaven on Earth. Love, joy, peace, abundance, health, happiness, hope, are all yours.

"All power is given to me to be meek and lowly of heart. I am willing to come last, therefore I am first."

Linda's Story: The Perfect Plan

Working with the Divine Energy is like cleansing the body. When I was cleansing, I would find that just when I was really starting to feel good and my body was strong – BAM – another layer would surface, kick me in the butt, and I would have to begin cleansing again. I would be tired for a while. Then the strength would come back. Then the next layer would surface and need to be dealt with. And so on, layer after layer. The interesting thing about cleansing is that it got easier and easier. Pretty soon it didn't knock me for a loop anymore. I would just feel a little tired, and eventually it didn't bother me at all. Each layer got easier to release.

Spiritually, it is the same way. When you are first learning to work with the Divine, the lessons kick you in the butt. I often joke that the only way the angels could get my attention when I first started working with them was to use a baseball bat to knock me down, mainly because of my own struggle with the need to be in control. As you learn to work with Spirit and let go of control, it gets easier and easier. You don't have to be knocked down to learn the lesson.

You may often become discouraged, because when you start on this spiritual path your life seems to become more chaotic. It only seems more chaotic because you are being required to change the way you react to circumstances, which leaves you a little confused and feeling out of control. I refer you back to my analogy of throwing clothes into the washer – they must get very agitated before they become clean. So it can be with us. It's not so much that our lives get more chaotic. It's that our perception of life starts to change.

So you make a decision that you're not happy with the way your life is going. Circumstances have backed you into a corner, and you can no longer ignore how you feel. You may have tied yourself for years to co-dependency, alcohol, drugs, obsessive-compulsive behavior, being a workaholic, or any other of a myriad of ways to ignore your feelings of unhappiness and discontent. Somehow, sometime, it all catches up with you. So you cry out for help to someone... to no one... to anyone...to God. That's when the angels rejoice, because they have your attention at last.

When we finally decide to accept the help of the Divine Energy, we make a commitment to change how we do things, a commitment to have more faith, to let go of control, to allow for intuitive guidance.

We think we are ready for improvement, but still we struggle against ourselves and resist changing our old habits of how we react to life. To help us over this resistance, God will continually put in front of our face the exact issues we need to deal with. This means that until we master these new ways, circumstances will continue to crop up that will require us to let go of control and use our intuition more. Repetition is a great teacher. Perhaps your issue is to understand that it is the angels working in your life responding to the request of your higher self. Or maybe you don't understand that the vibration of the energy on the planet has increased so much in the past thirty years that you can no longer ignore that nagging irritation that tells you that things aren't right. Welcome to Earth, Spiritual Being!

The past thirty to forty years has been amazing for this planet. We didn't have our end back in the mid 1990s, as predicted by every major religion in the world. Instead we had our beginning. Through the prayers at that time of as few as five percent of the total population of the planet, our destiny was changed. More and more people now are looking for answers from the spiritual realm. The old ways of surviving and reacting don't work anymore. Instead we are being called upon to put aside our anger, our un-forgiveness, our guilt, our belief in lack, and instead, to ride the wave of love.

I once heard a quote by John Randolph Price, the internationally known award winning author, "If we would only love more, all limitations in our life would be gone." That is such a simple statement, but so very true. God is love. Not the kind of love that we humans normally think of, but an all consuming, unconditional love, not based on judgment but on acceptance. So if you have been feeling backed into a corner, bless it. The angels are working to bring you your highest good. What makes it all so uncomfortable is the struggle not to change.

There was the most wonderful feeling of peace as I sat on the porch that evening after I started my Healthy Lifestyles business and was on my own at last. I really felt like I had arrived, and could say, "Okay. I'm finally there. I am done." But let us not forget that the only constant in the universe is change. We never get "there." When we actually do get "there" we shed this physical body and head to the other side. In this life there is no "there." And learning that was a big surprise to me. I pretty much thought I was "there." Foolish me! I, like so many others, hated change. I wanted to find my comfort zone.

I wanted to be "there" in the groove where there are not ripples in the path. So for a while I lived with the illusion that I was "there."

Then the restlessness started again. Tiny things started to change. The perfect situation didn't feel quite so perfect anymore. Don't you just hate that, when you can't put your finger on what's different, but something has shifted? For a while you try to ignore it, but the uncomfortable feeling is there and soon, action, in response to an unsettling discontentment will be required. It's time to make a change. It was time for me to move my office to a setting that I felt would be more professional and to a better situation for me. Little did I know that I was starting a four year process that would include moving four times in two years, and would be a wonderful lesson for "going with the flow." Just about the time I would get really comfortable in my new location and situation, circumstances (or should I say, angels?), would have me packing up and moving again.

To keep my expenses down, I worked out of someone else's rented store space, which did not allow me much area or privacy for my own office. I longed for an office of my own. The only way I could picture this happening was to work out of my home. And the only way to do that, since I live in such a remote area, was to sell my house and move into town. Yes, that was definitely the answer. I reasoned that not only would I have the office situation I wanted, but it would cut my overhead for the business. I have always believed in being unlimited because God is unlimited. But as I look back now, I was being unlimited in a very limited way. Let me explain. We see a situation – a difficulty – and we work it out in our heads how this difficulty can be solved, put on blinders, look straight ahead and attempt to go directly to that solution. In my case, putting our house up for sale and moving to town was the only way I could see to have my office in a secure place, free from the whims of landlords.

I also wanted a few other things, and since it is good to be very specific with the universe, I made a list: for me, an exercise room with wonderful exercise equipment, and a big new kitchen; for Jessica, a big walk-in closet and an area where she could entertain her friends; a garage with a workshop for Scott for all his man toys – motorcycle, boat, four- wheeler, etc.; for the business, a place to keep herbs for the products that I make; and, of course, the office. I put our house on the market almost immediately.

However, we did love where we lived. The house was in a high demand area, very nicely located in the woods, but near a country club setting. It was really nurturing for us and Jessie had spent her whole life there. So as interesting as another place sounded to her, she was reluctant to leave. But as far as I could see with my blinders on, moving was the only way to go. For eighteen months we waited for someone to buy our house. We buried a statue of Saint Joseph in the front yard (that's supposed to help sell houses), I had the home Feng Shuied, I took down all personal items, and had a yard sale of stuff that had been stored for years. In short, we did everything realty agents suggest will help to sell a home. But there were no takers. As a matter of fact, there weren't even any lookers! I was really frustrated. I just knew I was on the right track to getting my own office. I needed my own office. I felt blocked, perplexed, angry, and confused for a year and a half! Finally, I asked the angels, "Am I looking at this wrong? Could I be missing something?"

DUHH!

When Scott and I began to look at the situation in other ways, the ideas started flowing. What if we refinanced and remodeled our house? Could we make it work with all the wants and needs the three of us had? We decided to try. We applied for a new mortgage in order to use some of our equity to finance the remodel. We had the money within thirty days. Piece of cake! When all the dust cleared (literally), and the remodeling was done, I looked around and saw we all got exactly what we wanted...except my office. Everything else was done but for some reason we kept putting off fulfilling the need that had started everything: that office at home.

Enchanted Changes

I had moved my office many times, and it was now located in a shop called Enchanted Forest, a nice little metaphysical store. It was a very nice set up with my office in the back and the overhead was low. The store worked well because the owners and I both benefited. I got clients from their traffic and my clients bought their merchandise. It was a good combo, but with the remodeling at home finished, I wanted to focus on having space of my own for my office. I liked the store situation but it had some drawbacks, not the least being that I couldn't control the store hours or the merchandise it carried. It was June and I had been in the store a year.

I was at home doing dishes, my head blank as usual with this simple task, when I heard this very clear voice say to me, "The Enchanted Forest is going to close." I, being the very spiritually grounded person that I am, did what all spiritually grounded people do. I whined.

"Oh Man! I don't want to move again. Where am I going to go now?!"

As a matter of fact, I whined all night. I went to bed and actually fell asleep whining. At 3:00 A.M. I woke up hearing it again. If you haven't read *Healing with the Angels* by Doreen Virtue, please get a copy. In the back of the book are number sequences and what they mean when the angels are trying to communicate with us. Well, the number sequence "300" means that the ascended masters are trying to tell you something and you're not listening. (Doreen actually says it in a much nicer way in the book). But I wasn't thinking about the number sequence right then. I just started to whine again. Only this time I caught myself, and the fear this message had generated. Fear always seems to gather in the pit of my stomach like this big heavy knot. It's not a comfortable feeling. This time I got it. "Okay, angels. Take away this fear and show me what I am supposed to do." I immediately felt calm and a scene popped into my head of a store – an angel and fairy store. I saw the location and what was inside and I thought, "So the angels and fairies want a store of their own! What a grand idea! I can have my office in the back, and it will be mine." As I lie in my bed, the angels and I began a planning session:

~ 133 ~

"I need someone to work with me. I can't work 24/7." So they showed me my friend, Veta.

"But," I said, "She must have the same vision as I do regarding the store..." More scenes, more questions, more answers. On and on the angels and I went until we had gone over all of the details. My fear was gone and replaced with new excitement. I was in a new adventure! Finally, I closed my eyes and slept without that lump in my stomach.

The next day I called Veta and I asked her if she was ready to open a store. She screamed, "It's about time! Of course I am ready." We met for lunch that day and talked out the details. As the angels promised, our vision was the same, right down to the name of the store: "Wings of Light." We sat there together. It was the middle of June and we both wondered when would this happen.

"You don't think the angels want to open by July 1st, do you?"

"I hope not. That would be crazy. How could we get everything together in time?"

It was a little scary because in the new energy, when it's time for something to happen, it usually happens fast. I went to the Enchanted Forest and asked the owner if she planned to close the store. Her answer surprised me. "No. Not at this time. Things are slow. But I am taking it one day at a time."

I called Veta and told her what happened. We were both a little perplexed. We thought for sure this was the time. We put the vision for the store out there and now it was up to the angels to figure out how to do it. I wouldn't compete with the Enchanted Forest, and to tell you the truth, the thought of moving was not on my list of most fun things to do. So I let the whole thing go.

One week later, the Enchanted Forest owner came in to my office and said she was closing the store and I needed to be out by July 1st.

A Time to Receive

Could I move out and reassemble my business in time to be open in just ten days? If I had not been given the information a week earlier that the Enchanted Forest was closing, I would have been at a severe disadvantage. But the details were now already in my head. I just had to act on them. One of the details the angels and I talked about was the location of the store and the availability of space. I called the landlord of the store I wanted to rent, and of course the space was available because the renter was moving out! Everything had been arranged nicely by the angels and things were set for me to move in. One glitch, though. The soonest we could move in to the new space was the same weekend as the White Mountain Women's Club Fashion Show. I freaked! Not only was I one of the chairpersons in charge of the event, I was also the commentator. No matter what, I had to be there.

The next ten days went like a whirlwind. I can remember feeling that I would never get all the details together, and the angels kept saying, so calmly, "Just take care of what you need to do today. Take one day at a time." Okay. Have you ever opened a store? Well, I never had, either. How about trying to get a carpenter during their busiest season to come in at the drop of your hat? We did. And that, my friend, has got to be Divine! Things flowed together right down to the building of the office in the back. The store was open for business and I was seeing clients in my own office by July 2nd. When those angels want something, they sure move Heaven and Earth to make it happen. And I have had no reason to regret it.

Once the whirlwind finally calmed down and it all came together, I sat and contemplated everything that happened. I received all I had asked for. My home nurtures my soul and has everything I wanted. I have my own space for my office and it is actually better than I had planned. I am able to supply my clients with books and information from the store, all at my fingertips. And I get new clients because the store draws them in.

But none of this came as I thought it would. It probably took a lot longer too, because I wasn't really thinking in unlimited terms. I was thinking with my blinders on. All of the things I received are far better than what my plan was. The only time it got really difficult was when I struggled against allowing things to happen divinely. There's that saying again, "You know how to make God laugh? Tell Him your plans."

Sixth Key: Forgiveness

I want to thank you for reading this far. I am humbled that you have found the information compelling enough to hang in there. Or perhaps you have reached this chapter by randomly thumbing through and have stopped here by chance. It doesn't matter because you are here for whatever it is you need, whether for one chapter, one Key, or the whole book. You are guided to receive what you need for your own journey. I am perfectly okay with that because that's how the Divine Energy works.

The last chapter was on Humility, and I think we all learned a little something from that, including me. How we are humbled from the power of God, the power of love that flows through the universe; that which keeps all the planets in place, but also flows through each and every one of us, including the casual readers among you.

Your perseverance has brought you to the sixth Key, "Forgiveness." When I was going through and writing down the Eight Keys to the Kingdom as the angels were giving them to me, I thought, "Oh, gosh. This is a piece of cake!" I got to "Humility" and was a little stumped by that. I thought that might be the only one that I would stumble on. But when I got to forgiveness, I thought, "Now wait." You can probably count on your hands a dozen times how many sermons have been given, how many books have been written, how many times you have heard about the importance of forgiveness. So I'm not here to tell you what you already know. I told the angels that I didn't want to sing that same old stale song; that you all know how important the subject is, and now you deserve to know what the next step in forgiveness is.

So we are not just going to talk about forgiveness. We're going to go beyond that, because this particular energy is so powerful. When you grasp the concept that is being brought to you here, "Forgiveness" is the one single Key which, if used alone, will change your life. Used with each of the other Keys, it will raise you in awareness and in energy frequency, to change your very soul.

Let's start with the people in your life that you have thought have done you wrong, people who you think have not given you the best of themselves, people who may have stabbed you in the back at one time or another. These may even be people that you love. You are not alone. This is the one area that most brings people to seek answers to their situations and issues. Many come to me to give them a quick and easy way to make those troubles go away. By the time they come to me they are at their last straw. The only thing I can say to them is, "You need to bring forgiveness into this situation."

And they say to me, "But you don't understand." They tell me I don't understand what this person in their life has done to them. I don't understand how this situation changed their life. They are so frustrated that, "Linda, you just don't understand," is blocking what they are willing to hear.

I can only answer that with, "Perhaps, I don't know that situation. But I want you to think now about how badly you've been wronged, and about how many years you have been holding on to that grudge, that pain, that anger, that insecurity. I want you to think about it, and think about that person or that incident that happened in your life that hurt you so badly. And then, when you have recalled to mind the memory of the pain that was caused you, when that memory is so real, and that pain is so intense that you can almost taste it, I want you to jump your thoughts over to this:

We are at the top of the hill. It's a cloudy day, maybe a little bit of rain. The wind is blowing, and we see a man there, who's got blood running from his hands, and he has blood running from his feet, and there's blood running down his face, because of a crown of thorns on his head. He's hanging on beams fashioned to resemble the outstretched limbs of a tree, called a cross at that time, by nails in his feet and hands. And just for fun, somebody is stabbing him in his side with a spear. As this man hangs there at the top of this hill, the energy in the world is changing.

You know what his words were: "Father, forgive them for they know not what they do."

"Father, forgive them…" I forgive them because they don't know what they're doing! I forgive them because they are in fear! I forgive them because they are in ignorance! Father, I forgive them. And if this man, who was so tortured, and so stricken, can say those words to the people who are around him who only want to hurt him, can you do any less? Do you really think that what you have experienced is any worse than that?

Oh, yeah, we can go on. Jesus was the Great Prophet, yes He was. He was the Son of God, yes He was. He knew the secrets. He understood them. And you, my friend, have no excuse because you also have that God energy flowing through you. You are also children of God. You are also great prophets in your own right. You have no excuse to be holding on to this energy that literally will destroy the cells in your body; this energy of unforgiveness. Now, think about that.

We come onto this planet with a path that we choose to follow. Before we show up here we get together with the angels, we get together with God, to decide what we are going to do in this go-around.

I have a feeling about those of you who are reading this book. I think that many of you came into this lifetime in order to make it your last incarnation. You made the decision that you want to "get it," finally. You want to get this plan, the spiritual understanding, this one last time. If you didn't want this spiritual understanding, you wouldn't be reading this right now. This book would not have appealed to you and I suspect that this is either not the first book of its kind, or the last that you will seek out. When you picked up this book you were looking to go beyond the norm. So, each and every one of you is seeking something deeper; something that will help to make this your last go-round. And that was the plan when you came.

Do you know what happens when you make this your last trip? You get all kinds of things thrown on your path, people, circumstances, things that come your way that are going to challenge you. So whether you believe you set this up for yourself or not – and don't confuse this with predestination, there is no such thing – there will be circumstances along your path that will teach you and help you to grow. These circumstances are created by you (your higher self), and God, so you can get the knowledge to look beyond the earthly way of doing things, so you don't have to come back again.

We have this intent in our spirits to understand more than we now understand. So even if I don't know your life's story, I know how hard it has been. And I do understand the roadblocks that have been on your path. I do understand what you have gone through. I may not have the details, but I get it. To tell you the truth, it's really not important whether I get it or not. I've got nothing invested in that. What's important is that you get it.

Yeah, you've had a rough road. There have been people on your path, circumstances in your way, challenges that you have had to face, and people have hurt you. Circumstances have hurt you. And some of you are still holding on to the things that happened twenty, thirty, forty, fifty years ago, with people that aren't even on the planet anymore! They've already left and you're still holding your grudge or your pain about that situation.

Now, think about this. Every situation that has been in your path has brought you to where you are now.

Do you think that you just pulled up the last ticket in line and you got all the stuff that was left over? Do you think that God said, "Oh, just throw 'em a bunch of junk in their path?" Do you think that it is just random that you have experienced what you have experienced? Whether it's emotional, mental, physical, do you really think it's just random energy thrown your way? It's not! We know better than that now. We've seen what God can do! We know the power of the Love Energy, as it has created this planet and has created miracles in so many people's lives. We have the Eight Keys to the Kingdom, the Kingdom of Heaven on Earth. If you cannot hold this Key called Forgiveness you will be outside the door, forever stuck. It's not a punishment. It's a choice; a choice that you make.

Forgiveness needs to happen. Jesus knew that. Those were His words! Forgiveness needs to happen to have the Kingdom! You cannot hold onto those angry feelings, that unforgiveness, and expect that your life is going to be just full of God and full of love. You will have God, you will have love, make no mistake. God does not keep his love from anyone. The energy is always there for you. However, you will be settling for quite a bit less than the share you are entitled to. You settle for partial love, partial joy, partial peace, and partial abundance, not the complete, because you choose to withhold yourself from your full measure. Without forgiveness you hold yourself back, you choose to settle. I encourage everyone not to settle, ever. In order to experience the true Kingdom of God we must move on. It doesn't say love, joy, peace, abundance, and anger.

So on this path called "Your Life" there are things and people along the way that have brought you pain in some form, maybe many forms. And you may still be dealing with them or they may have moved on to the other side. What are you going to do with that feeling that you have been wronged? What are you going to do with that anger, those hurt feelings? As long as you continue to hold onto that energy, you will continue to be the victim of that pain, and you will continue to have that negative energy working in your life. There is no way around that because, just like a magnet, you will attract back to you the energy that you put out. Is it really worth holding on to?

Why was I born to the parents that I was born to? My mother was a manic depressive. My father sexually abused my sister and me. It took me a very long time to learn what I am telling you now: to hold no grudges for what was done to me; to love them as God loves them. They're both gone now, but if my father and mother had not been who they were, I would not be who I am today, speaking to people of angels, writing this book for you. The challenges that my parents brought into my life, the pain, the agony, the lack of self esteem – that journey that took me from that little girl who was abused to where I stand today is the only reason that I am who I am. It is because they were who they were, and did what they did. I bless them. It took me a long time and a lot of effort to heal. But now, I bless them.

The reason I do what I do, stand up and bare my soul and my past to strangers, other than to keep my promise to God, is to help each of you to understand that you too, can forgive. That you are not as different because of your issues, your challenges, as you think you are. There are more of us in the world than you ever dreamed there were. We, the people with scars, and the people with wounds still not healed to scars, can forgive. Jesus forgave to show us that we can, too. We can bless those who gave us our challenges, as He blessed His challengers.

Somebody is going to come into your life and they're going to be the bad guy. Someone is going to step into your life, they are going to look you in the eye, and you're not going to like what you see. Somebody is going to step in and make you feel small and bad. These people who make you feel miserable, who make you feel that your life is a failure, are your angels! Get used to having these people in your life, because your energy brings them to you. They put in front of you exactly what it is that you need to deal with, what you need to face about yourself. They are there to make you ask, "Why am I upset; why does this person have control over my life; why am I not succeeding; why am I not moving forward...why?"

Do you really think that anyone has that much power over you to make you miserable? They don't. No one has that much power. You always have the power over yourself.

I have another story, because I am beginning to sense that you love my stories.

Many years ago, a large organization that I volunteered with on our mountain put together a fund raising luncheon. The committee I ended up on consisted of one other lady and me, because we felt better doing it together, neither of us having done anything like that before. We wanted to come up with some creative ideas for the event. Probably because it was my first experience doing something so large, I made a few mistakes. One was that I asked a friend to cater the event for us. The friend really didn't want to do it, but we talked her into it. We wanted her because we knew she was really good. So, she gave us a price that, although fair, reflected that she really didn't want to do it. We accepted her price and she agreed to do it.

However, the price that she gave us was not acceptable to the sponsoring organization, and after several weeks, they told us they had gotten someone else. I had to go to my friend and tell her. But because this was a very large event and catering was required for around three hundred people, my friend had already reserved the date in her schedule. To say the least, she was very angry with me. She was so angry that she still has not spoken to me to this day. She was angry because our delay in telling her of the cancellation caused her to lose other business, an even larger group event. She was angry because our cancellation was her financial ruin. Our event was for four hours of one day, and there was a bigger group event that she could have scheduled on that same day, during those same four hours. One day out of three-hundred-sixty-five days in a year, with the same four hour time frame. Is that coincidence? No. She lost that deal, and she lost our deal. To this day she will tell you that her business was financially ruined because of what I did. Does anyone, do I, have that much power to ruin anyone financially? Or do you think that maybe there was Divine Energy in what brought that together for her? What issues did she have that could have contributed to her "financial ruin?"

Now, I am as human as the next person, and I went through weeks of guilt wondering what my part in all of that was, and what I could have done differently. I felt very bad about the situation for a very long time. It was never my intention to harm anyone, and it took me a while to get over it. After I was able to get through my mental and emotional debris connected with this issue, I was able to look at it and see the divine at work. Obviously, the angels brought that conflict, that energy, into her life because she attracted it to her. She must have been in conflict already about her business, or she would not have received it.

You can blame whoever you want for the "failures" or trouble in your life. It's quite possible that this person will go to her grave thinking that I ruined her business life. Blame whomever you will. But it doesn't change the fact that the trouble happening to you needs to be examined from a personal point of view. Why is this person in your life? Why was this event in your life? Why are you experiencing this trouble? Why are you going through this heartache? Get it back where it belongs, right there with you, right there in your own heart center.

Oh, I admit there are some people out there who really do have some antagonistic personalities and are out to do you some mischief. We see them all over the world. They think you do them wrong, they want to do somebody else wrong. It's in my T.V. soap opera all the time. If you want to get information on how to totally screw up your life, those are the kinds of things you want to watch. Because they take every negative emotion, amplify it ten times, and put it right out in front of you. It's a good lesson in "Oh, I'm never going to do that!" But I have to watch. It's a little like a train wreck. It's awful, but you just have to watch!

Life really doesn't have to be like a soap opera, even though there is always going to be someone in your life who's not going to agree with the way you're doing things. There are always going to be circumstances that challenge you. You came into this world with that already scheduled. Face it. You brought it with you. Expect it. Understand it, so it doesn't knock you down every time it happens. There is Divine Energy in every step that you take, and as much as I was dismayed at having to be the catalyst to bring that issue up to that person, to be in that uncomfortable position. Someone is always going to step in to be the bad guy. The world, unfortunately, still needs bad guys. That time, it was me. Sometime it will be you, or happen to you. Even the bad guy is part of the divine plan, because the bad guy makes you think, makes you hurt, makes you feel. When you feel, you are alive. And when you are alive, God can speak to you so you can turn the hurt around and be strengthened in the way you need to be strong.

Understand that we are not just dropped off here. We are not left to fate. People are in your life for a reason. Understand that, so you can let go of the hurt, the wrong they did you, the failures, the troubles. Let it go!

There are people who come to me for counseling who are fifty, sixty years old and they're still mad at their mother from when they were four. Some of you out there may identify with that. It may be your issue. We hold on to these things. "Oh, I could never succeed in business because my mother didn't give me this opportunity, or that opportunity…!" Or, "If only my mother had sent me to dance school…I really wanted to dance. I mean, I have to move."

Do you really think that God just opens this window a little crack and you miss an opportunity? Do you think that anyone out there can keep you from missing your opportunity? Do you really think that one person could really be your financial ruin, your emotional ruin?

There is always, always a reason. But, and understand this, you may never know what that reason is. You may never know why this circumstance, or these issues, those people, have come into your life. You may never know why. That is why we have the Eight Keys to the Kingdom, and why you need to Believe, and to Trust, to Detach, and to send in Love. It's a big world out there with a lot of people to deal with, and you will be dealing with them daily for the rest of your natural life. Are you going to hold a grudge against the gal at Safeway who was in a bad mood the day you were there because something happened in her life and she was rude to you? Come on. But people do it! Haven't you ever heard, "Oh, they were rude to me. I'm never going into that store again." We've all said it, but you don't have a clue what that person was going through. You don't understand!

We don't need to make that judgment. Maybe the only reason you were there, at that moment, was to smile at them. Maybe that was your mission that day. And instead, your ego got in the way because she was a little rude, or she was upset, or whatever. Your ego gets in the way and says, "Huh! I don't have to take that. I'm not going to go back there, ever," when all you had to do was bring in a smile and a thank you. "Thank you for this service, even though I know you don't want to be here."

We live in a very, very, interesting world, and because you have chosen to read this book, you have made a conscious decision not to live your life the way everyone else does. Maybe you didn't know that when you bought it. Maybe you didn't know that when you opened the cover. Maybe you didn't know that you were telling God you were ready to go beyond the physical world. But God has said, "Ooh! I'm going to take you there!" When you make the decision to take in this knowledge you are going beyond the physical world.

So look beyond now. And I want you to think about those people in your life that have harmed you, that have hurt you, that have allowed their egos to get in the way, that maybe had prompted your financial ruin. And understand that those people have no power, other than what you choose to give them. They have no power in your life, and you are holding on to unforgiveness, anger, anxiety, fear, disbelief, lack of self esteem, pain, and injury. It's not hurting them. It doesn't harm them at all. What it does is create physical changes in your body. Anger, unforgiveness, fear, all those negative feelings, create negative physical changes in your body. Those changes will age you faster, your body won't digest as well, your heart won't beat normally. These changes will allow disease to creep in, and eventually, after long battles with dire illness brought on by this negativity, these changes will kill you. Please try to understand the harm you are doing to yourself.

It was not worry for my mother or my father that made me begin to forgive and to let go of the injuries I received from them. My letting go of what they did to me, or did not do for me, had nothing to do with them. I let go and forgave because I needed to be free. In order for me to have the Kingdom of Heaven on Earth I needed to be free. You need to be free. You need to be free of those negative emotions that will kill you and, at the very least, kill your spirit.

Now, God gives you everything you need to be free. Everything! There's no random act, there are no coincidences about the path that your life has taken. None. Somewhere along the way, your higher self has made an agreement with God that it's okay for some trouble to be thrown into the mix. If you are on your last go 'round here – and only you can examine your spirit for that – then you can expect that a lot of things will come up, because you have to clear them. You have to clear these energies out so that you "get it," so that you really understand why all the trouble you get comes to you, why those energies are important to you. Then, when you go home after this go 'round, you'll be home for good. I think that most of you are saying right now, "Oh, yeah! This is my last time, my last show in the Bigs! I want to 'get it' now!" If you want this to be your last hoorah, prepare yourself, because that "to do" list of things you need to clear before you can go home for good may be very long; so many people in your path; so many things you're not willing to look at. Of course you can choose to come back. That's your choice too. But, if that intent is there to make this your last go 'round, understand that it will be even harder. We are the one that tells God when we want to go home, when we want to make this our last trip. And She will know that you are choosing it, and that you are ready for everything She will send your way.

A few years ago, when I wanted to sell my house, I decided to take out all the unnecessary stuff. You know how we just pack things away? We don't need them, but we don't want to get rid of them either. I started taking things out, not only because I wanted the house to show better for sale, but to also clear the energy attached to all that stuff from my past. So I brought this great big trunk out of the attic that contained stuff from back in high school, papers, report cards, little mementos, graduation tassel. This was stuff I had shoved in this trunk more than twenty-five years before and carried around with me all those years. My daughter, who was eight at the time, was sitting there while I was going through these things, and I found some letters from old boyfriends. We were both reading them and all the letters pretty much said the same thing. They were mostly notes from young men saying, "Sorry I was such a jerk...sorry I was such an idiot... sorry I was a bonehead." Jessie, after reading maybe ten letters all saying the same thing, asked me, "Mom, did you just date jerks?"

Well, I was a little taken aback, but after thinking a minute had to admit, "You know, I think so." They even told me they were jerks. They informed me they acted in a stupid way. They told me in this "Gosh I was really stupid, I shouldn't have done that" way. And I continued to date them! We can be so totally blind to the people that come into our lives and hurt us, and I was so hurt by every single one of those relationships.

Jessie said, "Jeez, Mom! What were you doing?"

I get it now. I gathered up all that stuff that seemed so important at the time to hang onto and store away, all those memories of the past, the pain they represented, and I threw them away. And then I forgave all those young men. And I also forgave myself, because I took it on! Those guys were even telling me how bad they were at the time, and I still accepted it from them.

So I'm asking you, "What are you doing?" Come on. Clear all that old stuff out. Clear the energy of all that old stuff. It doesn't need to be in your life. We are going to go through a meditation about forgiveness, a very powerful meditation that will help you clear all that old baggage you have been carrying around. But I want you to remember that it's not that people aren't going to come into your life to challenge you. It's not that circumstances are not going to be created that will cause you to feel a little uncomfortable or a little off-balance. You will always have that. But what these Eight Keys to the Kingdom will give you is the strength to understand, the strength to get through it, the strength to believe, to trust, to detach, to love, to forgive, and to be humbled by the power of Spirit.

There are always going to be those people who don't like you. There are always going to be those people who cut in front of you in traffic. There will always be people who are jealous of what you have, or want what they think you have. There will always be someone who will need more than you can give, and people who you will always let interfere with your good coming to you. That's not going to change. How you react to it, what you choose to hold on to, what you choose to release – that, my friends, is what you can change. And that's what will change your life.

So let's get into that meditation now.

I was talking to the angels about this meditation for the book because it's a little longer than what I have been using. But they want you to have it because it's a very, very important exercise. If you can do this meditation every night for the next ten days, the energy that you will clear will be absolutely phenomenal.

Meditation #6

Take yourself to a safe place, a place where you can go that's all yours. It can be real or not. And I want you to feel or visualize yourself standing in this safe place. Picture in front of you every single person in your life who's ever hurt you in any way, shape, or form. You should have a pretty good crowd.

There's the person who cut you off in traffic, and the person when you were five, the little boy next door who threw mud on you; anyone with whom you have ever come in contact that has offended you, that has made you feel bad, that has made you question yourself – anyone that has hurt you.

Some of the faces you'll actually be able to see and know. Some of the people you won't recognize at all. Some of those faces you won't even see, because they are people you interacted with only once and may never make contact with again. These people have hurt you in some way or another and they are standing in front of you right now.

I want you to send them forgiveness, every single soul. Send them love, send them forgiveness. Forgive them. Forgive each one. Forgive them all.

I don't care how many there are, forgive them all.

Bless them for the part they have had in your life.

Forgive them. Wrap them up in a big bubble, that whole huge group. Wrap them up in a big pink bubble. Pink signifies love. Fill that bubble with love. Breathe love into that bubble so that each of those souls is completely surrounded by that love inside that bubble.

Now send them off to God. Lift that bubble up and hand it to God. Send it now. Send everyone in that bubble to God.

So, the field in front of you is clear now. You've forgiven, you've wrapped them in a pink bubble, you have surrounded them with love, and you have sent them off to God.

Now, my friend, comes the hard part.

Now, standing in front of you is every single person you have ever hurt. Every person you have said a rude word to, every person you were nasty to, every person you've cut off in traffic, every person you were short with because you were tired, or late, or grouchy, every person you've ever made a judgment about, every person you have talked about; anyone whom you have put negative energy into their life during your entire lifetime. That should be quite a few people standing in front of you, crowds of people.

Some of the faces you'll see and know, and recognize. Other faces you won't. Some faces you won't even get to see at all. They will be blurry, but they crossed your path somewhere along the way and you caused them pain, whether intentionally or not.

And now, you ask for their forgiveness. Ask for forgiveness.

It comes to you automatically because of the energy of intent that you sent out. Because you ask, because you want forgiveness, you are forgiven.

And now wrap this group in a pink bubble, breathe love into the bubble, and send it off to God.

And feel the clearing in your heart, and feel the energy grow around you.

If you will do this every night for the next ten days you will clear out whatever energy, whatever karma, whatever you have created over your lifetime. It will renew your spirit and will heal your body. It will free you. You will be free.

Now take a minute and just relax, and feel the freedom that came from clearing out all of that old stuff.

Linda's Story: Lessons from the Angels

Hebrews 11:1 from the New Testament tells us that, "Faith is the substance of things hoped for, and the evidence of things not seen." I have heard this over and over in my life. What a true statement. But what happens all the time is that we get in our own way. All we need to do is see the end result in our hearts, what we really want, and let the angels take care of the details. And they prefer that we don't tell them how to do it!

Put your thoughts together based on your true heart's desire. See the end result, and let it go. Do not set timeframes. Divine timing is much different than ours and works much better than we ever could. Wayne Dyer says it perfectly: Expect everything and attach to nothing.

Letting go is a key to living an abundant, happy life, free from stress and worry. So what is it about us that makes us feel the need to force things to happen, or worry when they don't. Many of us feel we don't deserve our good. We believe that God can do miracles, but not for us. We keep a list of "should haves" and hold onto guilt, and a list of "shouldn't haves," harboring resentment, and believing all the while that we are undeserving of good.

God is not judgmental. We always seem to put God in human terms, only bigger. So if we love, God must really love. And if we get angry, God must really get angry. God is not human and we shouldn't relate to Him as such. God is the energy of Love; all encompassing; all accepting, which means without conditions. We hold the judgments on ourselves and perpetuate that feeling through our experiences, because what we send out is what we get back. If we send out judgment or guilt, the energy comes back to us to validate our feelings, and then we think that God is punishing us. When we change our thoughts and release our judgment or guilt, the energy will come back to us more positively.

I wish each person could see themselves the way the angels see them, the way I see them through the angel's eyes. The angels always see the best in us, our potential, our creativity; our pure spiritual selves. We are spiritual beings having a physical experience on Earth. We are all worthy and all capable of living happy, healthy lives.

When working with the Divine Energy, expect the unexpected. Let go of attachments to outcomes and understand that work in this energy creates new avenues that we, as physical beings, could not even begin to create. I had a vision of what I wanted. It was really not my desire to leave my home that nurtures me, but I thought that was the only way to accomplish my goals. Luckily, the angels are not limited, as I am. I thought I had to settle, give up something I loved in order to have something I needed. We do not have to settle, ever. When we honor ourselves and our needs, the whole universe supports what we do. It is up to us to realize what we deserve and want. We cannot depend on others to meet our needs or wants. That only leads to disappointment, especially since most of us don't even know what we want anyway. Let go. Let go. Let go.

Our thoughts have a direct effect on circumstances in our lives. It is always a choice for us how we react to any particular situation. When I had just quit the insurance business and started my own practice, I received in the mail a bill from the community counseling center I went to years earlier. The bill totaled $200, not an excessively large amount, but considering I had just left a job where I earned more than half our family income, any amount was large, especially when I didn't have it. It was Friday afternoon when I received the bill, so I had all weekend to worry about it before I could make a call on Monday morning. I had health insurance that covered counseling for the dates of service listed, but I knew I did not have the receipts. However, I made a choice. I chose not to worry about it. After all, I was doing the work that the angels had led me to, so I assumed they would take care of my financial needs.

Yes, it was just that easy. On Monday morning I called the counseling center. They were putting in a new accounting system and were going over the old unpaid bills to try to update and collect. The bill I received was never paid, according to them. (Okay, some panic began to slip in). I explained that I had insurance that should have covered the bill. The gal at the counseling center said, "Okay, that's fine. We were just checking." End of story. Done. Just like that. They never billed me again.

Maybe this story would be more impressive had it happened more dramatically, if I had actually owed the money and a check showed up in the mail the next day for the exact amount. Divine Energy doesn't always work dramatically. Sometimes, most of the time, it is done with little gestures, like this one. It really doesn't matter though, whether it's done with drama or with easily overlooked simplicity.

What does matter is that the issue was all taken care of, and not by me. How simple is that? How easy was that?

On the other side of the coin, when you hold on and send negative energy into a situation it just adds more fuel to a negative fire. On the days when I let stress get to me, when my tiredness gets the best of me, especially now, while I am discovering how to do menopause gracefully; when I know I should stay home and nurture myself but it's not always possible, I find myself butting my head up against negative situations one right after another. I know my energy creates the situations. Like when you are standing in a long line at the grocery store, when it seems that everyone is checking out at the same time, you can decide to get stressed and have a miserable five minutes tapping your foot, twitching, doing the heavy sighing thing, until it's your turn. Or you can take a break, read a magazine, and relax. It will still only be five minutes. It's all about choice. When I get home on those stressed days, I look back over my day and feel incredibly stupid for having acted the way I did, too much energy wasted on negativity. What's the point? You make it simple or make it complicated, but you choose.

I know it seems like I am over simplifying things and perhaps that is so. But we have to be aware of our thoughts and what triggers them. How do your parents and friends view life? What habits have you learned from them? It is important to understand that how we react to life is habit, and if any of you have ever tried to quit smoking, or sugar (my monkey), you know how hard habits can be to break.

So now, with this knowledge, you can begin your own awareness and realize you can control your reactions to life.

A Time to Heal

Depression can be an overwhelming condition. It is a disease that will rule your life. There are many medical treatments, anti-depressant drugs, which do what they say they will do – depress your true emotions. None of us likes to feel insecure or powerless, let alone dwell on it and admit it. But if we do not examine how we are feeling, we will never get to the bottom of the real issue, the real things that make us depressed.

I have reached a point in my life that when I start to feel uncomfortable or threatened by situations or people, I pay attention and examine the "why" surrounding it. It hasn't always been that way. After having worked through so many of my issues, I now deal with each as it comes up. But before this I was dealing with thirty-plus years of issues. Many people have more years than that of holding in their emotions and pain. How do we get over this? How do we move to a place of peace? Self examination is so important in that process. We must face what it is we fear most: ourselves, because more often than we like to admit, we direct our anger, which is generated from that fear, at others, usually those closest to us.

I can remember times when my husband would come home from work, obviously glad to see me and greeting me cheerfully, but I would feel angry at him and want to just slap him. It wasn't him I was angry with. But it was him I wanted to take it out on, even though he had done nothing wrong, and I was never one to actually take out my anger with physical violence. I caught myself and knew I wasn't angry at him, but that didn't diminish the anger.

You are reading this book most likely because you are looking to improve or to heal some part of your life. And improvement, and especially healing, cannot take place without looking at your issues of anger and unforgiveness. We cannot be spiritual without being forgiving. We cannot rise in vibration when we are possessed by unforgiveness. We cannot heal and be filled with unforgiveness. This is the most important issue we have to face. At the base of our fear, anger, and guilt, are our unforgiven issues. Whether our need is to forgive ourselves or others, we must deal with it.

A Struggle for Power

There are many authors that write about a forgiveness inventory. There are many books written on this subject alone. So you can see how important forgiveness is. At the heart of depression is the issue of unforgiveness. Think of all the people in your life that have hurt you and that you have hurt. Think of the times in your life when you have given away your power to someone. Do you understand what it means to give away your power to someone and what that feels like?

My daughter had a wart on her finger that she wanted removed. Due to so many health issues in my past, my comfort level in a medical doctor's office was almost nil. But Jessica wanted that wart removed, and I was more than happy to take her for the procedure. I had depended upon alternative medicine for the whole of Jessie's life and a doctor's office had become a foreign place to me. I felt off balance the minute I walked in. I recoiled like a child, as the front desk staff scolded me for not having my daughter's immunization records with me, and then when they scolded me again for not having brought her into the doctor every two years for a wellness check. Jessie was fourteen, at the time and had been healthy her whole life. But I let them make me feel like such a neglectful mom! I gave away my power as soon as I walked into that office, and everyone knew it.

It was necessary to come back the next week for another treatment, so I scheduled a wellness check for Jessie. Once again, walking in, I gave away my power and it was another uncomfortable experience. The last visit, I got wise and made it a point to examine my feelings. I also asked the angels to intervene on behalf of Jessie and me to make this experience positive for us both. I understood that my insecurities about being a good mom were brought up to the forefront by just stepping into that office. Once I realized what I was doing and what was being triggered, I was able to make it a positive experience.

Now I can recognize the feelings of being insecure, but before, when I was in the throws of my depression and zero self-esteem, I spent most of my time giving away my power to men, friends, bosses, and family. I wanted everyone else to see the value in me because I couldn't see it myself. What does all this have to do with unforgiveness? Everything.

Until I realized that I was angry at my father and could accept that anger and forgive him, I was a prisoner. When did you first give your power away and to whom? You may have to think back to when you were a child. I gave my power away at a very young age to my father, and I tried to get it back numerous times with other men in my life. I would set myself up in impossible relationships, trying to get them to approve of me. I wanted to be worthy in their eyes. That, of course, could not happen because I did not believe myself to be worthy. They were just reflecting back to me how I felt about myself. Once I was able to take my power back from my father, by allowing myself to be angry, accepting who he was and forgiving him, I no longer had impossible relationships with men, either personally or professionally.

They say that animals can sense our fear and it is important not to let them see it. If animals can sense our fear, then you can bet people can too. The interesting thing is that most people don't realize it on a conscious level. When I walked into that doctor's office with no power, they were all over me about one thing and then another. How could they know I was feeling powerless? But when I walked into that office with my power, those same people were so nice and accommodating, I was amazed. Once again, it all comes back to us. It comes back to the choices we make.

Medicating with Meditation

Forgiveness is a huge issue for your healing, but before you can forgive you must figure out with whom you are angry. I have worked with many clients that do not allow themselves to be angry, especially at their parents. The belief is that it's not right to be angry at them, or there is the belief that the parents did the best they could. All grown up, we can look back and say, "Yeah, my parents had it really rough. They couldn't help it."

My mother, the manic depressive, had a habit of flying off the handle and beating us. But hey, she was a manic depressive and couldn't help it, right? As an adult we can make many excuses for people's behavior. But when I was six or four years old and being beaten, I didn't understand what a manic depressive was, so I just figured there must be something wrong with me. This is the part that hurts and feels unworthy, the six-year old inside. This part will remain unworthy and hurt for your whole life if you allow it, which means that there will always be that part of you that gives away your power.

When I work with clients, I take them through meditations that take them back to the time when their power was lost. Sometimes that is as far back as two or three-years old. I have their adult self watch their younger self and what was happening to them at that time. I literally encourage them to become angry at the injustice done to them as a child. Getting angry shows that you believe you deserve better. It is the start of self-esteem.

Let's say you heard on the news of a child being beaten, a young child. You would be shocked and appalled. You wouldn't say, "Oh, that poor mom, she is a manic depressive." You would know what happened to that child was not right. It shouldn't be any different when reflecting on the source of your own pain. For me, I realized that the beatings my mother gave me when I was a young child were not my fault. Neither were the violations by my father. They were the adults! They should have been protecting me, watching over me, making sure I was safe.

In sessions, I take these meditations further and have the client, as the adult, intervene on behalf of themselves as a child.

This exercise is to show the client that as the adult they now have the power to rescue and take care of their own inner child. Once the child has been rescued, the next step is to visualize a safe place for the adult client and child to go, a place where no one has power but them. Then the client visualizes the offending person standing in front of them both, the adult and the child. I encourage both adult and child to release their anger at the offender, telling them exactly what they feel about how they were treated. The child and adult each get their turn to yell, kick, scream, holler, whatever it takes to release the anger they are holding onto, even to the point of visualizing themselves beating up the abuser! Remember, this is in a meditation, and words are not spoken aloud but the release is tremendous. When both child and adult run out of anger, when no more angry words come to mind, when all the angry energy is spent, then the way is open for forgiveness.

I then ask the client if the child and adult are ready to forgive. If all the anger is gone, forgiveness will come naturally. If they cannot forgive, I have them go back and do the exercise again to release the rest of the anger. Forgiveness allows you to release yourself from the energetic and karmic ties. After the forgiveness is spoken, then the offending adult is visually wrapped in a pink bubble and floated away to God.

This procedure for releasing anger and forgiveness may need to be repeated several times as layer upon layer of anger is released. I can't even count how many times I had to go through it in regard to my father. There were many times I mentally and emotionally beat him to a pulp before I felt I could forgive, before I could surround him in that pink bubble and send him to God. I would wake up angry and ask myself who I was angry at. Sure enough, it was my father. So I would again do the meditation. I finally released all the anger at my father some time ago and have accepted him for who he was. I am free. To some this may seem like a long and arduous process. Perhaps it is, but not as long as taking the unforgiveness and anger on to your next incarnations and having to deal with those souls again and again, until you finally release that negative karmic bond. If you desire to release your anger, you will be surprised how quickly this process can help you accomplish that.

This meditative procedure is so positive because you get validated. I have had many clients ask if they need to confront their abusers in person. I adamantly advise against it, first because memory is very selective and people have a tendency to forget things over the years, especially the more painful experiences. And second, to have a confrontation in this kind of situation only puts the offending adult on the defensive. And face to face confrontation can actually backfire and end up making you feel even worse, because offenders usually are pretty good at making you feel responsible.

The purpose of this meditation is to free yourself by disconnecting from the energetic ties to your past traumas and abusers. Using this procedure of forgiveness you get your power back, you connect yourself with your inner child and you are able to be whole. Then, when you eventually encounter the offender, you will be surprised at how your feelings toward them have changed. You will have a totally different relationship with them because you will no longer feel the need for their approval. There was a time when I would get on the phone with my dad and still long for him to tell me I was wonderful. After I released my anger and fear toward him, I could have a conversation without seeking his approval, or anything else from him for that matter. We were just two adults having a conversation. We were done with our karma. I will not have to spend any more lifetimes working through issues with him. I believe he still has issues, but I won't be on that merry-go-round with him ever again.

You can still do this exercise even, and especially, if the offending adult has crossed over. Usually, but not always, their spirit is looking for forgiveness too.

I followed this procedure for various offending people in my life. Then I did a group forgiveness of all who offended me, and all whom I may have offended in my life. This clearing is amazing and important for us all to do. You don't need me or another professional to follow this procedure and accomplish forgiveness. Just follow the steps and set your intent. The angels will lead you.

Seventh Key: Gratitude

The summer of 2006 was one of the rainiest on recent record for our mountain. The forest loved all the moisture which turned the trees deep green and made them glisten with jewel-like droplets caught in their needles. The meadows were a pure delight, vibrant with brightly colored wild flowers of purple, yellow, and orange. As I was on my way to present the seventh key, the "Key of Gratitude," I was ooo-ing an aw-ing, cranking my head from side to side, completely amazed at the beauty of it all. I thought, "Oh, yes! This feeling inside is gratitude! Look at all the beautiful flowers, the sparkling water splashing in the creek, the sun rising through the clouds!" And then I thought, "Oh, get real!"

Yes, it's important to smell the flowers and appreciate nature, but that kind of gratitude is not what the angels want me to tell you about now. Most of us have to deal with a lot of negativity through the course of our daily walk on this planet. And if we get an opportunity to stop and smell the flowers, that's a good thing, but that's a subject for another day. Every single one of us knows how to be thankful for the beauty of the world, for the kindness of strangers, for the blessings in our lives. We always take the time to appreciate and marvel at those situations that seem to work out in our favor. This, too, is not what I am to address in this chapter.

What the angels want you to think about now is all the not so pleasant things in your life, those things that you are not so grateful to have to deal with – the people at work that drive you absolutely crazy, your employees that just can't seem to follow through on what they need to follow through on. Or maybe it's your teenagers that sometimes make you wonder why you ever wanted kids, or your financial issues that seem insurmountable, or the health obstacles you need to hurdle. That is your real life. The angels want you to find gratitude in all of this "real life" that you have to deal with day after day.

Finding gratitude in what upsets our lives is a foreign concept to most of us. To get started, let's take a little mental trip. Set aside all the feelings and perceptions of the events in your life that you think have hurt you; that you blame or give credit to for making your life harder, unhappy, or painful. Now do the same with your concepts of spirituality. And lastly, suspend your ideas about how you are supposed to live life. Come with me for just a minute and imagine that, at this very moment, we're in Heaven sitting in a classroom, getting ourselves prepared to go to Earth. The angels are giving a lesson:

> *You know, when you take on a physical body, there will be a lot of changes you will have to adjust to, but one thing will remain the same: you will continue to have an energy that flows within you. Now don't let it confuse you, because it's the same energy you have now sitting here in Heaven. We angels want you to understand that this energy is God, which you know here as the Energy of Love. That energy flows through the whole universe, is the same energy that keeps the planets in place, keeps the earth blooming, and is the energy in each and every one of you. We call that energy within you your 'soul.'*
>
> *Here's the tricky part: life can be very distracting, and once you take on your physical body, you won't consciously remember any of this class, or having been here in Heaven at all. To make things even more interesting, you're going to be pretty blank about what's going on around you there on Earth and you will have to start from scratch again, no matter how many times you have been there before. But we want you to understand that you will never actually be alone, although your earthly awareness may think so. You are connected, just like everyone else, to that Love Energy, and with each other.*

So the angels' lesson for us is that we are each connected by this energy. It brings a whole new dimension to the concept of "we are all one." Despite our differences physically, emotionally, politically, religiously, we are all connected by this energy of infinite love. As a Girl Scout leader to a group of twelve to fourteen girls, I used an exercise to illustrate our connection to each other. All of the girls formed a large circle and tossed a ball of yarn randomly to each other, each grabbing hold of the unwound yarn until the ball was completely undone. Every little girl had a piece of that yarn, and a weaving had been formed in the center of the circle that looked like a giant web. When one girl moved, the whole group was affected. If a girl moved left, all the others were compelled to move left. If one stepped back, the others had to move with her. They learned, not only the concept that we are all connected, that we are all one, but also that we are more alike than we are different. The girls saw how one person's actions affected everyone else.

The angels want you to understand that we are all connected to each other by a web of that incredible God energy, that energy which flows through you, and does not dead end in you. It is a two-way flow, both in and out, in a continuously renewing river of connections. The real benefit of this is when you realize it, accept it, you can work with the energy, and then see how God works to weave beauty and synchronicity into your life.

We have already talked a little about how our thoughts create our reality. If you are learning this for the first time, know that our thoughts are energy. We send them out and they attach themselves to "like" energy and bring that energy back to us. In this way our thoughts create, or manifest, what we want and need in our life. Whether our thoughts are negative or positive, they create what we have in our lives. If you're sending out negativity, you're going to get negativity back.

I once had an acquaintance who said to me, "Every time I go to a restaurant I get a terrible meal." I can attest that this was true for her. Every time we went out to eat, my meal was fine, but something was always wrong with hers. She sent that energy out and that's what was returned to her. Because we all are connected, that energy flows through each of us, even to those people in the restaurant. If she believes that she's going to get a lousy meal, she is going to get a lousy meal.

Let's go again to that classroom on the other side. The angels are explaining:

All of our energy is connected, so if you choose to go to the planet Earth and be negative that could be a real detriment. This could make it really tricky for you, because negativity is going to bring in more negativity.

But our connections also make it possible for you to have miracles. You can use our connections to enable God and the angels to weave for you an incredible tapestry that puts you in the right place at the right time to receive your 'seemingly impossible good.'

When you go to Earth, when you're in that physical body, you're going to have health challenges. You're going to have relatives, and bosses, and friends with whom you disagree. There will be political policies, and Presidents of the United States to cope with. It's not always going to be easy to understand why negatives are occurring and how they occur. But you need to know in your heart, that you are connected to God and to every other soul on Earth, which means that every single one of us is connected to the President, to those people in Iraq, even the ones who don't like us. We are, even every single one of us, connected to all those people trying to get the same parking spot at Wal-Mart!

What does this mean to you? Since we are all connected, we can make circumstances change. When we discussed the Key of Love, we learned that sending love into a situation will positively affect that situation. In that same way we can send love to a particular person, even to the President, or to a specific area of the world, because the same energy that flows through you flows through presidents, flows through the people who make you crazy, gets flowers blooming, and makes this world go around. Can we make it change? Yes! Can one person make a difference? Yes! This is what you need to be grateful for: That you are not here by any chance, there is no coincidence that you are here, or reading this book, or on this planet at all. You are here with purpose, you are here connecting with others. You are here to make a change.

What can one person do? One person can change the world. And this is what we are using our Key of Gratitude for. We are grateful that we don't have to settle for a world that's going to blow itself up. We don't have to live in that kind of fear, because the energy of just those who are reading this book, right now, can change that completely. We can change it, because we have that connection to each other and to God Almighty. We are connected to the most powerful energy in the universe, and gratitude opens the doors of all the possibilities in that universe.

Until you bring gratitude into everything that you do, your lines are locked, your door is closed. Gratitude is the key that opens up that door. You take all the other Keys we've been working with, and then you add Gratitude and the abundance starts flowing. I'm not talking about just financial abundance. I'm talking about healings and love. I'm talking abundance in the form of joy that is in your life. I am talking about all those things that make living worthwhile!

What is the point of being in constant emotional or physical struggle? God never meant for you to be in that constant struggle! God has meant for you to be in a state of joy, to have love, to be at peace, to be well, to live abundantly. He gives you everything you need to create that in your life. And for that you should be grateful. Why don't you have everything you need? You haven't opened that door to all the possibilities yet. The only thing that keeps you from having all of God's good is your attitude. Everything we need is presented to each one of us equally. Why are you struggling every day to make things happen?" God has placed everything you need on your pathway already. All you have to do is claim it.

The energy that permeates the universe is unlimited. God is unlimited. God's power is unlimited. God's good is unlimited. And you have unlimited access to it all. Love, joy, abundance, understanding, peace, healing for your body, your mind, your heart, your spirit; all of this is yours for the taking. The only price you pay for this is showing your gratitude for it being there for you. Show your gratitude by using the eight Keys given to you in this book. Be grateful for the doors these keys unlock.

Let's take one more look at the lessons the angels are giving us in that classroom on the other side:

Each of you, take out your contract form. You must fill in the blanks before you will be allowed to make the trip to Earth. Each contract is unique and is based upon what you have decided you need to accomplish for the growth and enlightenment of your soul. No one can make the decisions for you. The choice is yours alone.

Make sure you give yourself adequate opportunity to face the challenges that will strengthen your soul's weakest points. Don't forget to consider character and personality traits and flaws. That will help give more dimensions to your challenges.

We can't stress enough that the more difficult the challenges you set for yourself, the better your chances of giant steps in your advancement. Remember, your ultimate goal is to never have to go through life on planet Earth again. But beware of the small print. What you do not succeed with, you will be required to repeat. So be brave, be imaginative, and be careful out there.

And, oh yeah, when you get to Earth, you won't remember anything about your contract either.

This lesson from the angels is all about choice. You choose your life, your family, your friends, your difficulties, your opportunities. What you do with them is also your choice. Suffer, flourish, succumb, or overcome. It's all up to you. What you need to be grateful for is that it is all your choice. You are not at the mercy of any power. Even the most powerful energy in the universe insists that you choose to have that power work in your life. It is never imposed upon you. It is that simple: it is all about choice, and you are in charge of choosing.

There is a mantra that runs through every single chapter in this book: "It's supposed to be simple and it's supposed to be easy." If your life is neither of those, then you need to take a look at it. You don't need to suffer, to do without, to give up your dreams, to put aside your wants in order to get what you need. You don't need martyrdom. All of your hopes, needs, and wants have already been provided for. Quit being a doormat. Quit telling yourself that your life is never going to work out, because if you say it, you're right! It won't.

Every negative you have experienced in your life, every set-back, heartache, disappointment, discouragement, and frustration was there by divine design. It was there because you asked for them, or you attracted them to you. You set them up, and you made the choices that facilitated the outcomes. When you begin to see these experiences as blessings, you begin to understand that they were there for your best and highest good. Your advancement to enlightenment depended upon the choices you made in those experiences. They gave you insight, strength, and an understanding that you would otherwise never have gained. Everything that happens in your life, the pleasant and the unpleasant, is for your highest and greatest good. That is the very essence of what the Key of Gratitude is for.

I told you in the chapter on forgiveness about my own journey to understanding of the power of divine design. Being grateful for the horrors in your own life is not easy. But, believe me it is necessary in order to be healed and to be rid of the trauma they continue to cause you in this life. It is also necessary to be healed of them in order not to carry that karma to your next lives. The Key of Forgiveness and this Key of Gratitude, used together, can heal any of life's wounds if you let them.

I don't think anyone knowingly chooses to bring negative energy into their life. If your life has been a series of negative events, maybe you didn't know that you were bringing it to yourself. Maybe the reason you are reading this book is because you asked how to get the negativity out of your life. If that is the case, then this is your answer. You were supposed get this book, you were supposed to have this message, because this message is for you, or you wouldn't have it. Be grateful for the connection that brought it to you.

If me telling you that you are responsible for all your own hurt, unhappiness, and lack in your life makes you uneasy, then I am glad. Because what makes you squirm in your seat is what you need to hear and it's what you need to work on before your life can change for the better. Before I understood this, before I "got it," I squirmed in my seat many, many times. Whatever I bring to you I have experienced myself. And this stuff works. The angels are never wrong.

You are working with the most powerful energy in the universe. There is nothing more powerful than what surrounds you at this moment, because God and the angels are here to meet your needs, to take care of your heartache, to take care of your heartbreak, to take care of your financial burdens. Believe it! If you do not believe it, it won't come to you. If you can't be thankful for it, it won't come to you.

There's no magic here, it's just a simple fact: your good is already here. Your abundance is waiting for you, no questions asked. You have access to the source of all your good right at your fingertips. Your boss is not your source. An inheritance is not your source. Social Security is not your source. And the lottery is definitely not your source! God is the source of all abundance on this planet. Once you understand that, you bypass all the discomfort that you have been struggling through. Your gratitude opens up that flow and brings all your good to you. The sooner you start using your Keys, the sooner you stop wondering if it is going to work or not, and the sooner you will find out for yourself. The best part is that you have nothing to lose by trying, and everything to continue losing if you don't.

If you want to make changes in your life, to move forward, to have healings; if you want contentment, peace, and joy, it's time for you to let go of your doubt, your worry, your inaction. It's time for you to say, "God, I accept the gifts that you give me on a daily basis. I am grateful for the good that comes to me every single day."

It sounds simple, just to say that you accept and that you are thankful, and things will start changing. It is that simple. There is no struggle or great sacrifice demanded of you. It is not complex. There is a need out there to make things complicated. I hear all the time, "Linda, you don't understand...I have this problem....I have that problem...What about what I've done?...What about what I haven't done?...What about what other people have done?...How am I going to get by this stuff?...You don't understand!"

You're right. I don't. But God does.

Humans feel they have to struggle, to be victims, to make things complicated. We have been taught that all our lives. Let the struggle go. If you want simple and easy, I promise you that's what you will have, because I have it. And if I have it, any single one of you can have it. I didn't always have it. I had to learn to have it. And so can you!

That doesn't mean there are not going to be issues or difficulties. It doesn't mean that there's not a bill that shows up out of the blue. It doesn't mean your life will always run smoothly and that your relatives will all love you and treat you with respect. You're still going to deal with people who are difficult. You're still going to deal with those relatives. You're still going to deal with employers. And you're still going to have things show up that you didn't expect. That's why you are here, to experience life! How you choose to deal with those circumstances is your choice. That is the gift for which we are grateful.

You don't have to choose struggle, even if the world chooses struggle to get by day to day. All you have to do is watch TV for a short time to know what they are struggling against. Headline stories like, "It Could Happen to You," are aired every day, and advertised all day long. We are told in large headlines and with dramatic music, "You Need to Be Very Afraid." They will frighten you with what's going to happen to your Social Security, to your investments, in your schools, or your community, or any number of issues that really press your buttons of fear. By using fear they can keep control because they want to keep you coming back. And because you are afraid, you keep coming back in hopes of having your fears allayed, only to find there is more to fear! The name of the game is to keep you tuned in so they can sell you their programming, and their commercials. The truth is that fear sells. And fear is contagious. Fear can sell you on believing in something you don't want to believe in, like doubting your instincts, spending your money on products you don't need, mistrusting your neighbors, and even going to war.

God does not want you to be afraid. God doesn't give you anything to be afraid of. We can live totally displaced from what frightens others in the world and how they react to fear. Your experience of life, which can be filled with love, joy, peace, and abundance, is an experience that most people may never have. That doesn't mean it's not a reality. We need to be grateful that this knowledge is given to us so we can change our experiences, make them free of negatives. Be grateful for the opportunity to say, "I get it... I'll do it...Give it to me, I want it...I am grateful, God, for the life You have given me. It is a gift, and the right way to live it is in Your love, and in peace and joy."

That is the gratitude the angels are talking about. Now you can go smell those flowers and appreciate their beauty. And while you are doing that, step off the path of complications and victimhood. Separate yourself from those who choose to make life complicated, and those who choose to suffer. It's your choice. Every morning when you wake up you have a choice of how you're going to go through your day. Yes, you're going to get a wrench thrown in the works from time to time. But you have in these Keys, the tools to take care of those wrenches.

Here is a story of a wrench that could have had very negative effects: My husband, one of the kindest and most honorable people I know, employs fifteen people in his window and door business. His clients are very nervous people building dream homes and vacation hide-a-ways for themselves, or contracting for others. He has more stress in one ten hour day than most people have in a year. His construction schedule is usually very tight and errors can be enormously costly for both him and the clients. His response to a particularly sensitive situation recently was, "I asked the angels to come in and help me. I knew this client was really, really upset about their order. I completely understood what they were going through and I sent them angels. I surrounded the whole issue with love. I also understood that my guys in the shop who ruined that multi-thousand dollar order were under a lot of stress, so I gave them a pep talk instead of yelling at them about their screw up."

His guys redid the order. The client was satisfied. No one was fired, everyone was given an opportunity to make good on their error, and they all learned a lot from the experience. Everything turned out for the greatest and highest good for everyone involved. These types of issues happen when you are in business and can send a person around the bend. But Scott is a man who has learned how to tap into the higher energy. Instead of creating more stress and chaos in his business, he is bringing in love and using peace and joy to bring honor to the people that work so hard for him. If this can be done under those kinds of stress levels, any of us can do it under our own circumstances.

We have a lot to be grateful for. We are blessed with so much love energy. This is the energy of God that tells us:

"I empower you."
"I love you."
"None of you have to suffer."
"None of you need to live in fear."
"None of you need to be victims."
"You can heal."
"You can have abundance."
"Life is yours for the taking because everything you need is already on your pathway."

Let us be grateful for the ability to tap into the most incredible and powerful energy in the universe. That energy is given to us, resides within us, connects us to one another, and we each can put that energy to work in our lives. We need to be grateful that God opted to plan it that way. We are never left floating alone on this big blue planet with no options. Be grateful that there are always options.

Meditation #7

Bow your head, take a deep breath, and quiet your thoughts.

When you are ready, visualize the negativity that is in your life right now. Put a face or a name, or an experience on each negative image. Imagine putting each negative image into that backpack that is weighing down your shoulders.

Now, take off that big heavy backpack that's holding all that negative energy and drop it on the road right where you are standing.

Breathe a sigh of relief, relax your shoulders, and lighten your heart.

Raise your arms to Heaven and just say, "Thank you, God."

Let that attitude of gratitude flow through you, because everything you need is already on your pathway. Everything you need is there for you to have, to hold, to accept.

Celebrate in gratitude. Let that feeling of gratitude fill your heart and your soul and let it fill the room.

For a moment, relax and just glow with gratitude.

Linda's Story: A Walk through the Light

In the summer of 2004, I finally began working on the book the angels told me I should write. As it turned out, that was the summer my father decided to make his way to the other side. His health had been deteriorating for months. He called me more that summer than he had in the previous three years. I suppose it was because he was feeling his mortality. It had been twelve years since I had seen him when he came to Pinetop to see us in 1992. He didn't stay long because he couldn't breathe there. It might have been the altitude, but I think it was more.

Dad was hospitalized several times, starting in early June that year. Each time his condition was critical and doctors warned that he might not make it. After he was discharged from his first stay, we had quite a long phone conversation. When I got off the phone, I had the same thought I always had after speaking with him: I did not like him. A few weeks later Dad was back in the hospital, and once again, they didn't know if he would make it. I spent some time talking by phone to his partner of seventeen years named, coincidentally, Nancy. She told me what a wonderful man my father was, how he took care of her when she was sick, how he was always there for her. I sat and listened to her speak of a person I didn't know. She told me about how he felt about his mother, how he never felt his mother liked him, and how hard he tried to win her approval. She spoke of his devastation when his mother died. This was never the side my father chose to show me. I know he also didn't want me to see him in the shape he was in, balding, teeth falling out, and wasting away. His ego would not let me know him that way. To me he always seemed calloused, sarcastic, and bigoted. He made no effort to change that image.

Scott and I had some free airline tickets and thought we might go to Ohio to see Dad for a weekend, but the thought of spending an entire weekend with him was very unsettling, and I decided I did not want to go. Since we had not yet taken a vacation that year, we left it up to Jessie to decide where she would like us all to go using the free tickets. It took her some time to think about it, and when she finally made her decision, she chose Ohio, but not because of Dad. She wanted to see Cedar Point in Sandusky. Cedar Point is famous for having the world's tallest and fastest roller coaster, and she wanted to ride it. So, as the angels would have it, we found ourselves planning to head for Ohio. I called Dad to let him know we were coming to see him, but it would be two months before we could get there.

At the end of August Dad took a pretty hard fall which caused bleeding in his brain, and he went into a coma. That week I got frequent calls from the doctors because Dad had listed me as his nearest living relative. Although Nancy and Dad were together for seventeen years, they never married, so she was not allowed to have authority in decisions about his care. She called me to give me her input regarding his life support. She was hoping he would come out of the coma and back to their life together. The fact was, if he did wake up, he couldn't be his old self. There was most likely brain damage. She said she had been asking him to come back to her, but I knew that my father really wanted to leave this earth. His kidneys had started to fail and the doctor told us that dialysis was an option, even though keeping him alive was futile. Nancy and I agreed he would not want artificial means to keep him alive in a vegetative state.

I told her as lovingly as I could, based on intuitive information I was getting, that he was ready to leave, but he didn't want to go without her approval. She cried, but realized the truth in it and spent all the next day telling him it was okay to go. At three o'clock the next morning Nancy called, saying she had been notified that he would not last much longer and that she was headed for the hospital to be with him. I knew she was right. I could feel he was in and out of both worlds. As I lie down, trying to fall asleep, I felt a huge surge of energy suddenly in the room. I knew it was my father. He hadn't passed yet, so I urged him to go back and cross over and quit keeping all those people hanging on, and I went to sleep. It was 6:30 A.M. my time, 9:30 A.M. in Ohio, when Nancy called to say he had died.

I felt relief for both him and Nancy that the ordeal was finished, glad that he had chosen to cross over. He didn't want to be here anymore, and I believe in my heart he didn't want to face me. I had long ago forgiven him for what he had done to me and my sister. The problem is I do not believe he ever forgave himself. Our trip to Ohio was to be an opportunity for him to make things right, but he was too frightened to face me or himself. The kidneys are where we hold our fear, and it was the failure of his kidneys that made his body finally give up.

That morning, after I had gotten the news, I felt his spirit just wandering. Later that same morning, I was given a vision where I saw my father standing at the end of a tunnel ready to step into the light. It was a good feeling knowing he had found his way. I haven't heard from him since.

Life on the Other Side

Over the years I have talked to many souls who have crossed over, and have begun to understand what happens once we reach the other side. Each of us is met by the angels once our spirit leaves our body. For some, the transition is as natural as can be. For others, especially if death occurs suddenly, the transition can be really confusing. When we first leave our body our personality from this life goes with us. The angels are kind, and lovingly go over our lives with us to help us understand and make the transition smoother. Once on the other side we are surrounded with love. There is no "big, bad God" ready to pass judgment and throw our souls into Hell. The energy is love, which is what God is. And we are given the chance to review our lives to see what we have learned and how enlightened we have become.

Different spirits make different choices when they get to the other side. Each of us is given a choice to examine, learn and grow there, especially if we didn't take the opportunity for much growth on this side. I have communicated with souls who have chosen to remain in the heavy emotions that they took with them from this life to the other side. They are still bitter, or angry, or unforgiving, even though the angels give them plenty of opportunity to let this go. These souls will remain in a lower energy vibration until they choose to move into more enlightenment.

One of the most powerful past life memories I have recalled was one in which I had been a rather nasty person and was responsible for the death of many people. When I crossed over, the heaviness of that lifetime left me in the dark because of the guilt I took with me. I could feel the angels compelling me to come over into the light, but I could not forgive myself, which kept my spirit in the dark. It took a while and I finally did move over to the light, but I had to make that choice. Even on the other side it is about choice.

When a soul makes the choice to move into enlightenment the learning begins. All things are done with joy and total acceptance. When my mother first crossed to the other side, at first I felt her energy as "Mom." As the years have gone by she has chosen to become more enlightened and her energy is different, definitely not Mom any more, but this wonderfully loving Light Being. Her vibration came down to sit with me while I was writing about her in this book. She was making sure I got the details of her life right. I could hear her voice correcting me on some of the details. It was a nice feeling to have her so close. Even though it was so painful to lose my mother, I knew it was a great release for her. She is just much happier on the other side.

Homecoming

We finally did take that trip to Ohio, to Cedar Point. We had a marvelous time. One of the things I wanted to do was drive through the old neighborhood where I grew up in my home town, to go back to the house at 18818 Longview, where I spent the first eighteen years of my life. I had been back once before, but this time it was different. Both my parents had gone to the other side. I had also come to that house many times over the years in my dreams, and during a healing meditation it was even burned to the ground, symbolizing letting go of the past.

When I saw the house, I was struck with how different everything was. It was so small, the house, the yard, the driveway. And I had especially remembered the front lawn as a lot larger, since as a kid, I had to mow it. In the backyard had been a gigantic tree that was now gone. Standing there looking at this place, this icon of my past that I had held almost sacred, I realized just how unimportant the past was. I had worked hard to let go, and it meant nothing to me anymore. There was really no point to even being there. I no longer needed to visit that past. I was finally living in the moment, and that moment was a totally different world from the one I lived in that house. And I was a totally different person.

It made me wonder why people hold on so tenaciously to the past, as if we could change what happened. I can't change the horror that took place at 18818. But I can let it go and be free to live this moment to the fullest. I realized how blessed I was to have my husband and daughter, and the life we built together. We pulled away from that place and I knew I would never go back to Ohio again. I was truly getting my last look. This life is about now. This moment is all we have. My mother and father each spent their lives dwelling on what they wished their lives had been, letting the past create their present. Neither ever found the happiness they craved.

Death will find each of us sometime, somewhere along the way, and will only be the death of our physical body. Our spirit will go on. We will each be given the opportunity to examine how we lived our lives, not from a judgmental standpoint, but based on what we have learned, and if in the end, we finally "got it." I love my parents for who they were and am grateful for what they taught me. I would not be who I am today had it not been for the experiences of my childhood. I chose them to teach me in this life. And it was my choice to decide what I would do with those experiences. I am blessed to have known them. I am blessed to be me.

No Happiness Out There

What does it take to be happy? A fancy car, a lot of money, a prestigious job? I've had a constant search for happiness my entire life. Happiness was not something that was common while I was growing up. I believe my parents wanted to be happy, but it seems that neither was able to accomplish it in their lifetimes. The biggest lessons learned in my childhood were, "You always have to settle, there is never enough, and life is a struggle." With these lessons firmly embedded in my psyche, it's no wonder happiness has been a constant pursuit.

My mother thought that if she could get her mother to love her she would be happy. She sacrificed her own wants and desires, and nearly her sanity, in a life-long attempt to get Grandma to say, "I love you." She even died still trying.

My father spent seventeen miserable penny-pinching and loveless years married to my mother before leaving her to marry someone else who was wealthy. After seventeen years with that wife, he discovered that financial security was not happiness. Haven't we all heard the old saw about how money can't buy...you know? The next seventeen years he spent trying to figure out what went wrong during all those previous years. But no matter what conclusions he may have drawn, happiness still eluded him. He shared those last seventeen years with someone who really loved him, and I believe he loved her too. But by the time he realized it, his health had deteriorated and he slipped into a coma, where he lingered for the short remainder of his life.

How long are you going to search for something that is not out there? No matter how hard you try, or how far you run, there is still no "there." After the first time I went to college and had to quit due to financial difficulties, everything I owned fit into my car. I had no ties to any one place, so when things were too difficult and the adventure got too thin I could pick up and move to a whole new adventure, to a place where no one knew me. Many times over the years, long after all my worldly possessions could never again fit into a single vehicle, I would still get the urge to move on whenever things got too tough. These urges came all too often. At some point I finally realized it was just geography and I would still meet myself after all the dust had settled. Happiness is just not out "there."

I have spent much of my time out "there" looking for the happiness factor. I remember that first major purchase that gave me that incredible high and I thought it was happiness. But it wore off so quickly, and I needed to buy something again to renew that feeling. There are those of you who have battled obsessive-compulsive behavior who know what I mean. It is only now when I look back on that time, that I realize how much I relied on outside stimuli to get "happy." But happiness that comes from outside of you is only temporary because it is an illusion.

True happiness can only come when you accept that you are responsible for bringing that energy to you. You create the reality in your own life – your pain and your pleasure. Nothing can bring it to you and nothing can take it from you. Accepting this ability is the first step to achieving a life filled with happiness and joy – a life filled with blessings!

Eighth Key: Connection

As we begin to think about our last Key I can't help but think of the summer of 2006 as a celebration. The summer was coming to a close, and August and September had been gloriously beautiful in our mountains. There had been so much wonderful rain, followed by warm sunshine that brought out all the wild flowers. They had bloomed like I had never seen them do, and it's as if God was celebrating with us. It was easy to feel God's presence with so many vibrant colors displayed everywhere as if She were proclaiming Her charge over us, so that we would have no doubt that She was watching over our every need and dispelling our every concern.

I have told you that this message was made especially for that summer and that the angels asked me to pass it on to you. There's an interesting story that came out of the presentations at the Unity Church that so perfectly fits with the subject of this chapter, the "Key of Connection." This story illustrates what connections are all about.

Years ago the angels told me, "Linda, you need to write a book." I confided in you the fact that I am incredibly obsessive-compulsive. Being obsessive-compulsive compels me to take a request like that and make a point of doing it, no matter what. God Herself had commissioned me to write a book and I was going to get it done! There's only one problem with that. I hate to write. So you can imagine the dilemma I found myself in receiving a clear instruction like that, being obsessive-compulsive and hating to write!

I made myself absolutely crazy over this. I would sit and try to put something down, but nothing would come out. The more I pushed and struggled, and the more times I sat down to try, the more locked up I became. I would sit and stare at the blank page not knowing where to start. I felt so inadequate and incapable of making it happen. But I couldn't let it go. I was consumed with the need to do what I had been instructed. One night, I was so keyed up over this that I was having trouble sleeping. So I got out of bed and wandered around the house. It was between two and three in the morning and I ended up on the couch, crying because I was in such turmoil over the instructions that I couldn't seem to fulfill. I told God, "I am just making myself miserable over this."

And the voice of God said to me through the angels, "Let it go."
"But you told me I'm supposed to write a book."
And they said, "Let it go. Let go of the struggle. Let go of the turmoil that you are causing yourself, because God doesn't want you to be in turmoil. God doesn't want you to be in struggle."

I understand now why they gave me those instructions when they knew how I felt about writing. They knew I didn't want to do it because it would force me to come face to face with myself; to look the source of most of my obsessions straight in the eye, and to deal with my fears about disappointing God. If there is nothing else I have learned from the angels, I have learned that you can't disappoint God. It's impossible. God loves without conditions, so there is never a circumstance that will cause Her to withhold that love. Everything that is given to you to do, or that you feel compelled to do, God provides you a way to do it.

That night, after realizing this, I let go of my guilt, the feeling of failure, and my anxiety about doing something I didn't like and didn't know how to do. I simply said, "Okay. I'm not going to struggle over this anymore. God, if you want me to write a book, you're going to have to make it easy for me."

I also let the project drop. I just did nothing about it. You know how fast time flies, and the next time the angels brought it up was two years later. "You need to write a book." This time I said, "Okay, God. I think I'm ready for this. I think I can do it now." My heart was in the right place, but I was not anxious to jump right in. I had to spend a few more months procrastinating, which included getting set up with a computer. And we all know how long it takes to find just the right one and then learn to use it. I found a lot of reasons to keep me from sitting down to write, because nothing had changed the fact that I hated it and still do.

Finally, I had no more excuses and began putting words to paper – or more precisely, words on the computer screen. The first thirty pages came out pretty easily. Then, I began to struggle. In all, I got nearly sixty pages down. After that I started choking up again. I set the book aside for another year and a half, which brings us to the summer of the Keys. Some time that previous spring, the angels told me that someone was going to show up in my life to help me write the book. Then, in one of the classes I was conducting early that summer, BJ, a good friend taking the class, came to me and said, "Linda, I need to tell you that somebody is going to show up in your life to help you write a book." I smiled to myself at the effort the angels were making to assure me they were sending help, and at the not so subtle way they were making sure I knew they wanted that book, and soon! But I was very grateful and relieved for that confirmation, because it took a lot of pressure off of me! I could have confidence that I would fulfill God's request of me, at last.

At the beginning of the summer, after one of the presentations, a beautiful soul, Karen Gibbs, came to me from the audience and told me she felt absolutely compelled to approach me to ask if I needed someone to help me write my book. I have been in the angel communication business a long time now. But sometimes it still takes me by surprise how directly it works and that it does work. In my astonishment I could only say, "You're kidding me."

Karen said, "No. You are writing a book, aren't you?" She told me later that she thought she was giving me a "smart aleck comeback" to my reaction and that I probably thought the idea of a book ludicrous. She had no way of knowing how totally serious I felt about that book and how much I looked forward to her offer of help.

This story shows just how we are each connected by all of our angels, and how those angels work in the background weaving that tapestry of our lives. My angels told me to write. BJ's angels told her to reassure me that help was on the way. And Karen's angels urged her to offer her help. If you ever think you are not connected, you are wrong. It's impossible not to be connected. This incredible connection is responsible for the collaboration I began with Karen so that the message of the Eight Keys to the Kingdom, and those nearly sixty pages I struggled with, could be put into book form. Now you know the miracle that is connected to it. As these words are being written I have no doubt that after all these years, this book will get out there, and I am blessed to be a part of it. And I am blessed to have that beautiful soul offer her help to me because we always think that we are hanging out here alone. But we're not. The connection is always there. You are never at a point where you are not connected. You are never in a place where you can fail God. Miracles happen every single day, and angels are in your life every single day to put together whatever it is that you need.

In the chapter on Gratitude, we discussed how the spirit of God is in each and every one of us. His spirit is connecting each and every soul out there. And that's how this beautiful soul came to help me, even though she did not know I was supposed to write a book. God was able to send a message to this lovely lady that said, "You need to go help her. She's floundering on this little issue." And she heard the voice and she said, "Okay."

There is something even more astonishing about how the angels and God provided that connection that summer. Like each of us, Karen had her own issues for which she had asked God's help. Her impulse to offer help to me was fulfilling prayers she had made for the resolution of some of those issues. She had no idea that her own help would be coming through me and through the book. Four years earlier, Karen's husband had died suddenly, leaving her overcome with grief, not only with the loss of her soul mate and life companion, but also with an unexplained breach of relationships with all but one of her immediate family members. She had struggled for three of those years deeply distraught and wondering about the value of continuing her life. Unable to make more than a meager living, the fourth year she had become completely dependent, emotionally and financially, upon a daughter and son-in-law, and was living with them. For a strong willed, independently minded woman, that was just about the last straw. But something inside of her kept telling her to use that time to find a new focus. She began asking God to end her grief, to help her understand why her family went away from her, to bring joy back into her life, and give her a reason to live again.

In all of her sixty-something years, Karen had never lived away from family, but she was inexplicitly determined to leave her home in Phoenix to spend the summer in our town. Through friends in Phoenix she learned about the Unity Church in Show Low, and decided before she came that she would worship there. The first Sunday she attended services, she volunteered to help with the Alternative Health Expo taking place that coming week and the congregation immediately made her a part of their community, offering their friendship as if they had known her for years. She had never been a person to act on impulse and even shocked herself when she volunteered on her first day, and among strangers. But she felt strongly that she should.

She was part of the audience for three of the "Keys" presentations, and with each felt that it was more and more urgent that she speak to me. When she actually came up to offer help, she was very surprised to learn that I had actually started a book, but that it had been sitting on a shelf for three years! She thought her offer was just about the messages from that summer. She had no idea it was so much more. Being involved with the Keys to the Kingdom, learning about the kind of help I give in my business, Karen found a new direction for her life and new meaning. Transformed from an injured, lost, and displaced victim, she was recharged with enthusiasm for living, a renewed sense of purpose, a better understanding of why bad things happen to good people, and a rekindling of her deep faith. In short, she received through that one connection that summer, everything she had asked God to give her. This just goes to show that connections are multi-dimensional, working in many directions at once and do not stop at one person's door.

Connections work by bringing you in touch with people and situations from everywhere. The purpose is to bring everyone involved with that connection exactly what they need. I see examples of this every day. There are people who just wander into my store because they think it's a fun little place. They are surprised that it's not just a unique gift shop, but that there are a lot of services available. Many times I end up doing readings for them or giving them help with their health issues, providing services that they didn't even know were available when they walked in. One of my long-time clients is a woman from Texas who came in as one of those casual customers while she was on vacation in our mountains. I ended up helping with her health issues, working long distance after her return home, and she benefited from even that far away. She came a long way to make that connection, because God doesn't care about distance. She got what she needed and so did I. God has you connected to each and every one of us and to this wonderful energy. You can't miss! You can't screw up! You can't make a mistake.

Why do we need to be taught about these connections and that they are divine? Why isn't life just that easy for all of us? Well, like I said in the beginning, we humans have gotten caught up in the physicality of our lives and closed off that communication and understanding with which we all come onto this Earth. God allowed that breach because He intends for us to have choices. We need to make the choice to want that communication and understanding, and to invite His involvement in our life. To put any struggle into your life is foolish because it creates stress for you and the people around you, leaves you frustrated and angry, and closes your awareness to that connection. Trust your connection to the most powerful energy in the universe and keep it open. It is up to you to keep that channel of connection and communication open. Sometimes people come to me and tell me that they don't feel like they have that spiritual connection anymore. Nonsense! They always had it and it's still there. They just need to believe they have it and trust that it is always there, and be open to it.

What makes us think our connection is not there, or that it is not working, is that we get into fear or guilt, or we get into a place where we feel that we are not worthy. Fear is always going to be there. You need to understand that. And fear is not necessarily a bad thing, as long as it doesn't keep you from doing what you need to do. We are human and we will have fear. Bless it. It is a gift to you. It helps you see things more clearly. It helps you take steps that maybe you wouldn't take if you didn't have a little fear mixed in.

Guilt, on the other hand, is a totally worthless emotion that you need to get rid of, because it serves no purpose whatsoever. It interferes with your connection. Any guilt that you may carry with you, about whatever issue you may have, will block you from getting information from God. It won't keep you from being connected, and it won't stop God from communicating. But it will block you from receiving the information you need in order to move forward. So get rid of the guilt. It's worthless! You are all perfect in God's eyes, because you are a piece of God, and you are connected, by right just because you exist. So there is nothing that can disconnect you.

So let's talk about inspiration. Inspiration comes from that connection that you have with God. God is in you and anything that you are compelled to do in your heart, wherever your joy lies, God will create a way for you to do that. Anything that you are compelled to do, that is within your heart, that you have a passion about, is God's connection. Those times when you just can't let go of thoughts like:

"Gosh, I have to open up this store."

"Gee, I need to do this."

"I need to learn that."

"You know, I really feel compelled to take a trip to Hawaii."

That is God speaking through your heart center. It says, "Yes, you need to go. Yes, you need a vacation. Yes, you need to do this business. Yes, you need to do this for yourself." Whatever it is, whatever you are compelled to do is God speaking through you. So you are going to have everything you need to accomplish that task, even if God needs to bring in another soul to help you, which God will do quite lovingly.

There's never any judgment, so you need to understand your passion. Your passion for music, your passion for cooking, for art lessons, for bird watching, for writing a book, for...you fill in the blank...is a gift that has been given to you. And God will give you a way to express that gift. I don't know why they wanted me to write, but my dislike for writing is part of my own challenge to overcome. If they're going to give me a voice, they could have at least given me the talent to write. But it's my challenge. I accept it. I bless it.

So our connection, our inspiration to do things, to create things, to paint, to do any of those things that grab us and hold on – whatever it is – is your direct connection to God. And God is the biggest inspiration there is.

Every genius that's out there is inspired by God. Every simpleton that's out there is inspired by God. You will never get a great painter, a great musician, a great gardener, or a great street sweeper, who isn't totally connected to the spirit of God. When you are living that inspiration, when you are in that joy, you are connected. This book is God speaking through me. I get great joy standing up in front of a group and telling them about the angels and God's love. If they told me I couldn't do it any more I would be incredibly disappointed.

God's inspiration – whatever it is, wherever it is – you will notice it. We notice most the great geniuses. It is obvious in the Sistine Chapel, and you've seen it in great architecture. But it's in the everyday things where you see it the most. You see it in things like the best repairman in town, the most efficient and friendly teller at the bank, the quiet teacher that all the kids love, the guy that makes those fantastic sand sculptures, the guy everyone wants to paint their house. They are inspired to do what they do and obviously love doing it. It's all around! Just look in the bakery window at the great artwork there. And it tastes good too! Do you think one is more important to the Inspirer than the other, genius or simple worker? No. Inspiration is our connection, and when you are in that energy and are connected, this inspiration can't help but come through you.

So how do you get connected? How do we keep those lines of communication open? You are always connected. So the real question is how do you open up to it? You do that by saying, "Yes, God! What do you want? Where do I go? What do I do?" All you've got to do is say, "Yes," and the inspiration is there, because God is already hardwired into your life. It is up to you to choose to open up and accept that connection.

Then let go of being so intense! Quit taking life so seriously! We are here by divine pleasure. We are here because God has said, "Let me live life through you." There is a piece of God within every one of us. Enjoy the connection. Enjoy the flowers. Enjoy going to work and listening to all the people gossip and talk about everybody else. You can step out of it. You don't have to be a part of it. That's exercising your connection. Know that you don't have to participate in the negative parts of life.

We live in this world that takes things so seriously, where there is a constant cycle of fear, a constant need to feel guilty and a constant cycle of lack. But that doesn't have to be your life. You are connected to the very source of all the good that there is – God! Whether the need is for money, health, or joy, we are connected by divine right to that source. It is nothing you have to beg for. So don't get on your knees to beg God to notice you. You're already noticed. Everything you need is already on your pathway. You don't even have to ask. You just have to say, "Okay! I accept, God, because I know everything is there for me, because I am connected just because I am." Your connection is the eighth Key to the Kingdom. The Kingdom is being loved, having joy, peace, and abundance, health, and hope, all these good things. It is yours by divine right. So when I tell you don't take life so seriously, you need to understand. Don't take life so seriously!

People love to be caught up in dramas and traumas. Why is that? Something always happens in your life. You're always going to get those "somethings"– things that you had not planned. Some of you may hear from the IRS and you didn't plan it. Some of you may have some relatives or friends that are interfering. And you know you didn't plan that! There's always going to be that bill that shows up that you really didn't expect. It's okay. It's always going to happen. That's life. Get used to it.

Surprises typify life on Earth. There is no getting around it. The neat part about it is you have the connection. God said, "I'll take care of everything." We are advised by the Bible to, "Seek ye first the kingdom of God." So first open up your connection. Say, "Yes, God, I accept!" And then the rest of it is all going to show up. It says so. You can't deny that. Oh, you can try, and then you can make yourself miserable, and be with that group that likes to be in the dramas and traumas. But you don't need to.

Say, "I accept." And don't take life so seriously. God has a great sense of humor. Look at all the really funny looking creatures in the animal world. Have you ever seen a platypus? And how about those anteaters? There are a lot of really ridiculous looking creatures in the world, yet everything about them is functional. There is a reason for their funny characteristics. It helps with their survival. God created them and God created us. Do you suppose that to the animals we are just as weird and funny looking? I think that God knew that all his creatures on this planet would need something to laugh at. And we need to laugh at ourselves. Admit it! We are ridiculous at times. Look at how incredibly neurotic we are, all of us. I know when I say that, somebody is saying, "Yeah, you oughta meet my aunt! She's really..."

No, no, no. Bring it home, folks. I have worked with people one-on-one for many years, and every single soul has neurosis, every one of us. We all have our "stuff." And it is that stuff we can laugh at. I can laugh at myself. I know how obsessive-compulsive I am. I went on a shoe binge recently. It doesn't matter when you read this. I will have been on a shoe binge recently. Shoes and jewelry are my thing! I come out wearing a new pair of shoes and my husband says, "I haven't seen those shoes." And I say, "I know. It's the season when all the new styles come out, so you gotta have new shoes." He just says, "Oh." What he hasn't caught on to yet is the season I am referring to is "shoe season," which lasts twelve months a year for some of us! Nordstom's, Macy's, Wal-Mart. They all love me.

We all have our stuff. We're all neurotic and a little obsessive. Come on just face it, and let it be okay. Let it be okay, because it's what makes us each a precious individual. You each have your own incredible connection. Those obsessions that I have – my stuff, my neurosis – have brought me to where I am today. And I create in a way that nobody else can. You create in a way that only you can and that's why it's all so special. That's why the connection is so important. And all you have to do to activate your connection is to say, "Yes. I accept this, God. I accept that I am a little strange. And I bless it."

It is your connection. It is your uniqueness. It is what makes you special. When you say "okay," the passion comes through your heart. The passion makes you feel like you need to make something, to do something, to have something. You need to go somewhere, to see someone. Then the universe is going to supply you with what you need. Your passion is your direct connection to God. And that passion – I don't care what it is – will be supported by the universe.

As soon as you say "yes" you are in the moment. You are in the here and now, and then you can begin to receive God's communications, His instructions. The tricky part is not to argue with God. People always say to me, "Gosh, I wish I could hear and speak to God, speak to the angels the way you do." The only difference between me and most people is that I just practice it every day. Every moment of every day, you and every other soul, are sent messages. Most of the time, when you receive messages or instructions to do something, you will stand there – literally – and blow it off, resist, or argue with it. You will think that it's just your imagination, or it will not sound like a logical thing to do.

"It's not logical that I feel compelled to turn here when my plan is to go straight ahead. I always go straight here, and I am going straight now."

And sometimes when you look back at something that happened you say, "Oh, I knew that was going to happen!" or "I knew I should have done that." That was Spirit telling you to turn. "Well, I always go straight. You know how I always hate change, so I'm just going to go straight again." And then it turns out that you really should have turned. Quit arguing with God!

Early in the summer of 2006 I got a message about my daughter's best friend. She was a cute little gal, eighteen-years old, finishing up her last six months of high school. The angels said to me, "She's going to come live with you."

I said, "Oh no, that's impossible. She's got a home. She lives with her grandmother."

You see? I was arguing with them. "She lives with her grandmother, they have a great relationship. They love each other. She's just got six months more of school. She's not going to end up at my house. Ha, ha, you guys are so funny!"

Well, by fall of that year she was living with us. I had to laugh at myself. I thought it was so funny that after so many years of receiving information from the angels, I still say, "Aach, no, that's not going to happen." And then it happens. Presto change-o! I suddenly had a house full of young kids. I was actually beginning to enjoy the peace and quiet around the house, because the daughter had gotten a job and her own transportation. But suddenly they were all back at my house.

A funny and weird thing is that I had these angel cards, oracle cards, for sale at my store, and I would randomly open the deck occasionally to see what the angels had to say. More often than not the card said, "You have a connection with children and young people." And I'm like, "Aah, darn."

Then my husband said to me just before Jessie's friend moved in, "You know, I pulled a card out of that deck the other day. And it says, 'You have a connection with children and young people.'"

Okay, angels. They all came to my house!

The connection is there. The energy is there. Don't argue with God. Just say, "Okay." Spirit is in you, willing to bless you and give to you everything you need.

The Eight Keys to the Kingdom, that list of eight words given to me in the early morning hours of that summer morning, has been made into this book. The message was inspired by God, and evidently it's inspirational enough that it needs to be out here on the written page for others to enjoy. It's a simple message with simple words. And we all – you, the reader, and we, the authors – had fun with it, a little laughter here and there. We need to be willing to laugh at ourselves and be willing to accept others for who they are. It's all a part of that connection.

The Eight Keys to the Kingdom is a gift to you. All eight Keys are a gift. If you only read about one Key, that one Key is God's gift to you. Perhaps that one is the one you really needed. We are blessed every single day with this same kind of connection, this same kind of spirit that is within us. You are never not connected to Spirit. You are never not connected to God. If it's financial situations you have, if it's health issues you have, if it's emotional complications, or spouse issues, it doesn't matter! You are never not connected to God. And everything you need will be given to you to take care of those things. Everything!

You will be blessed by just saying, "Okay, God, yes, I'm connected, I accept that." It's all in the intent. And your intent to be connected, to be spiritual, is everything.

There are those that have been compelled to go into the mountains and sit and meditate 24/7. They get to hide out in monasteries, or someplace like the hills of India, and just meditate. It is said that they can actually make themselves disappear and reappear right before your very eyes. Everybody goes "Ooo!...Ahh!" And other people try to reach that point of spirituality. I don't really know if it's necessary to disappear and come in and out. But there are those that try and everyone says, "Oooh! They're really connected! They're so spiritual."

If you think that sitting on top of a mountain and meditating all day is hard, it's not. Anybody can be connected when they sit on top of a mountain, away from everybody else, away from real life, away from the pollution, from the relatives, from bosses, from politics, away from everything else "worldly." Anybody who sits around locked in a monastery all day can be connected. But to go every day to work, and continue to see the relatives regularly, to be a mom or dad or grandparent, to do what you have to do to stay involved with what's going on in your world, and still keep your connection open? That's a challenge.

The hermits and monks can be admired for stepping away from all the material stuff that this world has to offer and have people say, "Wow, look at them. They're so cool. They're so connected."

But, I admire you. I admire each and every one of you that take this journey, who are in the forefront, in the melee! You're enmeshed in it. You're working with people who are negative. You have unreasonable demands put on you. You deal with the unexpected that comes at the most inconvenient times. I admire you! I give you kudos. The angels give you a pat on the back, because you deal with it all in the middle of the spiritual, material, and emotional distractions of this world. You, who are searching for answers, who have read this message, are carrying that energy in your hearts every single day. You are looking beyond people's faults, bringing in the energy of God without ever saying a word. You're doing it just with a smile, just by a nod, just by the total acceptance of someone else.

Now that, my friends, is something! That is impressive, and you need to know it about yourself. Anybody can hide out and be connected to God. But what you have accomplished today, by choosing to read this message, is that you are connected to God. And you are in the world but not of it.

And that is what the Eight Keys to the Kingdom is all about.

Meditation #8

Take yourself to that wonderful safe place that's within your heart...your place, where you are surrounded by angels and you know God is always there.

You may find that your backpack has gotten a little bit lighter. But we want to get rid of it completely, because all your worries, and your cares, and your stresses are in that backpack.

All you have to do is say, "Here, I give this to you, God." Give it to the angels. They are asking for it now.

You don't want to haul that around anymore. It's too heavy.

Your path is supposed to be simple and it's supposed to be easy, and God offers us that.

We are connected by divine right to God. And whatever your issues are today, just give that intent to be connected.

Give that intent to allow your life to be simple... and easy...and full of joy.

Allow the Kingdom of Heaven into your heart. And all you have to do is say, "Yes."

Say "Yes," to God. Say, "I accept! I accept the path of love and joy and peace and abundance."

Take a minute now and just meditate on that.

Linda's Story: Love Me Tender

Throughout my life I struggled with the demons from my childhood that followed and haunted me. I was well into my adulthood before I learned of how my young life had been tormented by my parents, because I had blocked everything before age ten so completely from my memory. Only when I began clearing, in order to offer healing therapies to others, did I begin to learn of the traumas that created those demons. In the preceding chapters I shared with you how I dealt with those given to me by my father, and that I was able to maintain a loving relationship with my mother. I would like to share with you now, how I came to terms with my mother's role in the creation of those demons.

When I decided to become a spiritual therapist and to begin clearing, which means to discover and dispel negative energy within one's self that may block spiritual connections, I called Mom to tell her what I was going to do. She listened patiently and then said to me, "Linda, do not be surprised during your therapy if you find yourself very angry with me." She said, "I want you to feel completely comfortable to do that." I did not know what she meant by that. And I could only think of how hard my mother worked to support my sister and I after my dad had walked out on us when I was thirteen. I just said to her, "Oh, Mom, don't be silly. Look at all you have done! You are amazing. What could ever make me angry at you?!"

I had actually begun conventional therapy years before, learning to deal with my anger toward my father, which I thought was because he left us. I had carried that anger all of my life. Until I started the clearing therapy, I thought that was the only real issue I had with him. And in fact, I worked on that anger for many years. That conventional therapy did not reveal to me the abuse in my early life that was so well hidden within me.

Even before my father left us, my sister and I had become totally dedicated to our mother. She was the one person in the family who would give us a hug occasionally who did say, "I love you." After Dad left, Nancy and I were even more dedicated to Mom, and even became protective of her. We were just happy that there was at least one parent who loved us, even if that parent's emotional state was erratic and unpredictable. Mother's instability came in spurts and was diminished by the drugs given her by her doctors. We learned to cope with those manic depressive episodes without transferring her issues to ourselves. The physical abuse at the hand of our mother had ended for Nancy and me by the time I was six or seven years old, which was about the time we were old enough to not be so dependent upon her. But we learned to rely upon our mother because she was the parent that was there. She was a stay-at-home mom while she was married to Dad. Because he did not take an active role in our care, Mom was the parent we went to even when Dad was home.

After Dad's departure from our lives, Mom, Nancy, and I became closer because it seemed it was just us against the world. We three were all we had. We didn't have a close relationship to other family, like aunts or uncles or grandparents, to whom I might have gone for hugs and nurturing. I only had my mother and I knew she loved me. She told me so. She was not a warm person, but she showed me in many ways that she loved me. Many years into my adulthood, after I learned of her own childhood abuse and her lifetime effort to win her own mother's approval, I understood better the barriers that had stood between her and her ability to give her children love the way she really wanted to give it.

As I began my spiritual clearing therapy, memories and emotions of my father coming into my room began coming up. But there were more truths with which I had to cope and come to understand. I remembered images of my mother silhouetted in the doorway of my room as my father came in, and of her turning away helpless to do anything to stop him. Over time, dealing with these images and emotions, there was another look on her face I began to remember: relief. It was relief that he was not in her bed. Because of her own father's abuse, she was unable to give herself to her husband. She was frigid and crippled with terror.

I had to come to terms with my mother's failure as a parent, as a mother, to protect me. I had to learn how to deal with the anger and disappointment of that realization. I somehow never doubted that she loved me. But I had to find a way to protect that little six-year-old girl inside me. Because of the years of learning how to deal with the issues involving my father and learning how to forgive him, dealing with my feelings about my mother's failures came much more quickly, although not any easier.

I had to learn again, how I the adult, could protect Linda, the little child within me. I found the courage to mentally look squarely into my mother's eyes and say, "You screwed up," without feeling like that anger and confrontation was a betrayal of her love. I had to accept that I could not change the past any more than she could have prevented it. If she had felt she could, she would have. It was something "normal" in her upbringing to feel at the mercy of the men in the family. Her own mother did not protect her, nor had she protested. She actually added to the trauma by resenting my mother for being grandpa's victim. My mother did not lay that guilt on me. That was my father's specialty.

Sexual abuse victims feel guilt for many reasons, not the least being that their abusers tell them it's their fault. But how is a six-year-old girl responsible for bringing a grown man to her bed? She isn't! My father was guilty, not I. My mother was guilty of not protecting me! It takes someone who is really screwed up to allow that kind of pain to be inflicted on someone they love. And my parents were really screwed up!

I had to learn to forgive myself, and then to forgive the parents who betrayed me, failed me, hurt me, even when in the case of at least one of them, they loved me.

I did learn to forgive them. It was easier with my mother because I knew she loved me. And I had already learned the forgiveness techniques in working to forgive my father. During the time when memories began coming up about my mother, she was in a very vulnerable place, living with her mother and subject to continued emotional abuse. I wanted to confront her with my anger but didn't think that anything positive could come of it. However, I did bring it up to her gently and said to her, "I know now what you meant about getting angry at you." We were able to discuss my feelings, and although she never really felt free enough to share hers, she had a great sadness about her. The pain was just too deep for her. And in spite of years of her own psychotherapy, she was never able to face it and release it. Her eyes silently begged my forgiveness and I gave it to her along with my love. And we both accepted that that was as good as it was going to be.

My relationship with my mother remained strong for the remainder of her life, and I feel a psychic connection to her even after all these years since she passed over. Since developing my psychic abilities, I have been aware of my mother's spirit around me from time to time. She has even made her presence felt while I was writing about her for this book, in case my account was too protective of her. I know that my karma has been fulfilled in regard to the abuse we both suffered because forgiveness has taken place. Without forgiveness we are destined to repeat our experiences.

I am not usually a good subject for other psychics to read because I am heavily surrounded and protected by angels. But I asked my angels for the opportunity to be read by an unusually gifted psychic who visited our town as I was finishing this book. The angels must have decided that this person's insight would be beneficial and would validate me because they allowed her to "see" me. Without me telling her anything about me or my family, she told me that my mother's spirit had changed dramatically since crossing to the other side. She told me my mother's aura, when on this side, had been filled with grey and black "debris," much like shrapnel, but it was now completely cleared. She said my mother had been offered an opportunity to grow and advance spiritually on the other side and that she was now a very wise soul, helping others, and that she was always around me, watching over me. It felt good to know that I was not the only one to know this. She is there. And she is one of my angels.

Spiritual Beings

We hear questions all the time like: "Who are we and why are we here? What is the meaning of life? Who is God, anyway? Where is Heaven? What am I supposed to be doing here? Why do some people's lives seem blessed while others are filled with turmoil and trauma?" These are the questions that have come up in every generation, of every society since the human race first began to recognize that it was different from the other animals on Earth. Our generation, our society in our time, is no different. Here are the answers I have found to be true, learned from the masters with whom I have studied, and enhanced by input from the angels.

We, the human inhabitants of Earth, are spiritual beings having a physical experience. But, you may ask, what is meant by "spiritual beings?" Well, as I have said before, we each have a piece of God within us. We could call this the soul. We are all part of that "One Energy," even the vilest among us. The secret is to tap into that energy at the highest level at which we are capable. Think of those people who can heal others, or who have performed miracles, the master teachers like Jesus, Buddha, Mohamed, and others. What secret do they have that we don't? What makes them so special? There is only one difference between them and us: They knew who they were, and most of us have no clue of the God within us. This awareness allowed them to tap into the higher frequencies of energy, frequencies that are available to each of us. The question is how do we get there? In order for us to get to this higher frequency, we must first remember who we really are.

So who are we? Who are you? Just for the moment release what you think you know to be true about yourself and who you are. Focus on these statements and allow yourself to absorb them:

I am.

I am God.

I am God incarnate.

Just in making these statements you transport yourself to higher energy. You may even, for a moment, want to close your eyes and focus on the portion of God within you, the "I AM." If you can stay in that moment just a little longer, you can feel your spirit being lifted to a higher place, where there is peacefulness, a feeling of wellbeing and of connection, and at the same time, a vibrant resonance that you did not even know was there. This is the energy of God, the energy of love that brings the feeling of oneness with all things. This is the source of our power.

What makes it so hard to stay in touch with that power in the "I AM" is the ego, the earthly self. There always seems to be a battle with the ego that keeps us from experiencing the "I AM." It is the ego that has control of our lives most of the time. The ego is the part of us that puts us in fear, guilt, or anger; the part that says we are in competition with others or subservient to others. The ego is the part that wants to get revenge, or says we are better than someone else because of skin color, social or economic position, political affiliation, or religious belief, any "reason" that helps us feel superior, which gives the ego control. The ego wants to be in control of you and most everyone and everything around you. Think about this: The ego motivated Hitler.

We are all affected every day by our own egos, and very profoundly by the ego of others, especially if we are immature or wavering in our own convictions. My daughter, when in her middle teens, felt an aversion to all forms of religions and even to Christ, primarily because the kids at school were constantly telling her she would go to hell if she didn't believe the way they did. These kids were from differing religious backgrounds and dogmas. But each felt they were right and, of course, Jessica was wrong because she was not one of "them." Their concern was not so much about Jessie's salvation as about justifying their own choices. Their egos needed that justification.

One night, on the nightly news, there were protesters with signs that said, "God hates Fags." Feelings and thoughts like this are the work of human egos. God does not hate. God does not have our human emotions. The energy of God is purely love. The ego constantly separates us from others and God and unfortunately, works through many religions and belief systems to do that. We need to think twice before we claim an alliance to something that separates us from others, or brings condemnation to someone, or a group of "someones."

Remember, energy attracts like energy. The energy of ego is always in a battle to be in control. And what it wants to control is you and others through you. This energy is the lower or negative energy of chaos. There are people all around you – you may see them on the news, you may work with them, or live with them; they may even be your friends – people whose egos are constantly emitting negative energy, so they constantly receive negative energy back. I have known people that have more negative things happen to them in one month than happen to me in a whole year. They constantly seem to be in a competition of some kind. They act as if someone is going to take from them what they feel is theirs by right. Or their priority is to be first, be right, be a "winner," always come out on top. Some put others down in order to build themselves up. This is the ego at full control in their lives. As a result, their lives are full of chaos, surrounded by people – relatives, or so called friends, who are looking to create more chaos.

Another side of ego is that it can keep us in fear and make it easy for others to control us. This I know well, having spent over half my life in this particular ego place. I know what it's like to live in fear each day, not even knowing what it is that you fear. I was always waiting for the other shoe to drop. Every time the phone would ring I was afraid of whom, or what circumstance, it would bring to me. This is the ego at work. I am sure this is what some would refer to as the devil. But it is our ego allowing negative energy to control our lives.

I allowed negative feelings and emotions to command me because I didn't know better. I didn't realize that I had a choice. Even my Pentecostal experiences didn't offer me a solution to the powerlessness that I always felt. It seemed that the "Devil" always had more power than little old me, the worthless sinner. In an attempt to overcome the feelings of worthlessness and powerlessness, which was my very healthy ego dominating me, not any devil, I became obsessive about controlling everything around me. When things got chaotic, which was most of the time, I would have to work harder to wrestle them back into check. You know those people that have to control everything around them; their space, their life, people, money? I was one of them. That kind of egotistical (of the ego) obsession is physically and emotionally exhausting, and creates illness in our physical bodies.

I am spending a lot of time telling you the power of the ego because we need to realize where our thoughts are going. We each need to do a self examination of our own lives. Where do your energies get spent? Are you always living in the past or the future in order to feel in control? Are you afraid to make changes in your life because something happened years ago that didn't work out?

Are you afraid that someone will take away your good, or that you don't deserve good? We have all heard of people that will stay in an abusive relationship because it is familiar, and their fear of the unknown is stronger than their fear of the abuse. It seems crazy but we have all done it. Have you ever stayed at a job that you hated because you were afraid to branch off to the unknown, crippled by the fear that things might be worse than what you already had? Our ego will keep us going in circles for our whole life if we allow it. It will keep us in anger, guilt, fear, if we allow it.

Life was never meant to be lived this way. Many of you probably, like I, grew up thinking life was supposed to be exactly like this. That's what we were taught by example for the most part, and have had little else to rely on. That's the information the people who raised us had to live with. It's not their fault. It is just what they knew. We are now living in a time of higher vibrational energy and have discovered that an ego-controlled life doesn't work. It never really did. But we know better now. In this higher energy vibration the negative comes back at you faster than ever before.

Since what you send out is what you get back, watch out! When you send out fear, fearful issues are what you get. You will literally create more reasons to be fearful. Yes, that is right. We create this. Whenever there is fear you are in "ego mode" and your connection to Spirit is corroded. Fear is at the base of all the other negative emotions. Guilt, anger, sadness, they're all about fear. I remember the worst beatings I got from my mother were when she was feeling the most powerless and fearful. She would try to control her world by taking it out on my sister and me. She never felt she had power over her life. For fifty-seven years she unwittingly gave her power to others through the fear of not being good enough. My father was the same way. He spent his life in fear trying to be good enough. And I spent so much of my life living in their example.

This is the fate of many people out there. How do we break this chain holding us to our past, to the old ways of thinking? How can we become good enough for people to love and accept us? We don't. It is not your job to make people love and accept you. No matter how good you choose to be, or how hard you try to make someone else happy, there will always be someone who will be disappointed, angry, or upset at your actions. So what? There are people out there that are just looking for a reason to be offended. You know them.

You've spoken to them and most likely, when they walked away, you felt completely drained. What a waste of your precious energy.

Who are all these people you are trying to please anyway? You live with them, you work for them. They live next door to you. What gives them so much power? You do! Once again, we can be our own worst enemy. Putting your ego on the back burner is not easy, but it is the only way to get past the fear of not being accepted. Live your life as honestly as you can, not how you think others want you to.

The angels taught me a long time ago about having integrity in my life and work. I do my best and try to keep my word. I take care of myself and my intent is focused on good. When each client comes into my office for an appointment, I give them my full attention and all the best of my knowledge and skills. Having said this, if I can't please them...oh well. If I disappoint them...oh well. I know I have done my best. And that is all anyone can do.

Intent is everything. Intend to focus on good and good will come from that intent. However, remember there are people out there whose egos are just looking for reasons to be offended. And you just can't please everyone, no matter how hard you try. I have had experiences where I have given the session my best and the person has left totally unaffected. I can feel good about myself, however, because I was fully present and gave the best intent that I could. On the other side of that coin, sometimes miraculous healings can occur and a person leaves having been healed. There is always the opportunity for healing. It is up to the person receiving the treatment to accept the healing or not. Either way, I don't take credit. Nor do I take blame. I give the client the credit for being open to receive. That is their choice. God is the Source, and each of us is free to receive from that Source.

The spirit of God brings us together with love, honoring our differences. God is experiencing Herself through us in each of our different ways as male or female, black or white, gay or straight, enlightened or naive. When you decide – and it is your choice – to put yourself into the higher energy of "I AM," you become a part of the whole; you reside in the higher energy realm. You learn to love yourself, and that love brings empowerment that sets you free.

Post Log - The Angels' Gift

Well there it is: this gift to you from the angels, this message of the Eight Keys to the Kingdom of Heaven on Earth, and the story of my own journey to that place of healing where the Kingdom is a reality in my life. I know these Keys work. I see them work every day in the lives of my clients and in my own life. I struggled to learn them. I gave up many times. But I got right back in there and struggled again, until I "got it." I continue every day to learn more about how the Keys can work in my life and how I can better use them.

The gift is yours now and it is up to you to accept it or not; to choose if, and how, you will use it. It is entirely in your hands. But just remember one thing: there was a reason the angels wanted you to have these Keys. They were given for your best and highest good. The angels are asking you to dare to reach beyond your reality. They are asking you to reach for that Kingdom. Take it.

The Eight Keys to the Kingdom in Action

🔑 First Key: Believe
- "I choose to believe."
- "I choose to believe that there is a Divine Power bigger than I am."
- "I give sixty seconds of pure belief that the Divine Power can and will come into my life."
- "I choose to open myself to that Divine Power and invite it into my life."
- "I believe I can choose to have the Kingdom of Heaven on Earth."
- "It's all good."
- "It's all divine."
- "I believe."

🔑 Second Key: Trust
- "Trust is an action word."
- "I am Trusting God."
- "Trust empowers me."
- "I accept Grace into my life."
- "I give this situation to God."
- "I choose a positive outlook."
- "I expect change."
- "I do not resist this situation."

🔑 Third Key: Detachment
- "Thoughts create reality."
- "I let go of control."
- "I accept change."
- "Negative feelings are a habit. I give them up."
- "I expect everything and attach to nothing."
- "I am in the moment and I detach from the outcome."
- "I accept that God will handle everything."
- "I get out of God's way."

☝ Fourth Key: Love
- "Love is the strongest power in the universe."
- "God is Love."
- "I allow myself to be filled with Love."
- "God's message is love."
- "Love makes everything easy."
- "Love's solutions are simple."
- "I surround this situation with Love."
- "It's all taken care of with love."

☝ Fifth Key: Humility
- "I am awed by the power of Love."
- "God, I can't do this alone."
- "I don't know what to do."
- "I humbly give control to God."
- "I humbly embrace the power of God in my life."
- "I accept that it's not always about me."
- "All power is given to me to be meek and lowly of heart."
- "I am willing to come last, therefore I am first."

☝ Sixth Key: Forgiveness
- "Father, forgive them…"
- "Everything that has happened to me is divine."
- "I bless everything that has happened to me, and everyone who has touched my life."
- "I forgive everyone who has hurt me."
- "I ask forgiveness of everyone I have hurt."
- "I wrap all my pain, resentment, regret, anger, fear and un-forgiveness in a pink balloon of love and give it to God."
- "I cut the strings that attach that pink balloon to me."
- "I am who I am because of everything in my life, and I bless who I am."

⚷ Seventh Key: Gratitude

- "The energy of God flows through and is part of every-thing in the universe, therefore, the energy of God flows through and is a part of me."
- "I am part of everything and everyone in the universe and therefore, everyone is a part of me."
- "This connection provides me with everything I need."
- "My every thought and action, whether negative or positive, affects the universe."
- "Through this connection, the same energy with which I affect the universe affects me in return."
- "I am awed by the trust that God has given me to choose how I will use this connection."
- "I am grateful for this connection."
- "I celebrate in gratitude."

⚷ Eighth Key: Connection

- "Each of these Keys is connected. I use them together for my greatest and highest good."
- "I am connected to the infinite source of all good that there is."
- "Negative feelings interfere with my connection. I release them."
- "I am always connected to everything I need."
- "I am connected to God."
- "I am part of God, and God is a part of me."
- "I accept this connection."
- "I bless it."

Meditations from 8 Keys:
A Special Delivery Message from the Angels
Now available on CD

Linda West guides you through all eight of the meditations included in this very special book. Reinforce your learning with these meditations just as they were done in the originally recorded series.

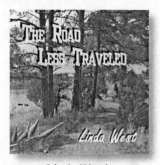

Linda West's
Meditations from 8 Keys:
A Special Delivery Message
from the Angels CD
$16.95

Linda West's
Road Less Traveled
A 1-1/2 hour CD presentation
$16.95

Available at www.lindawest-medium.com
Phone orders: 1-928-367-2040
Visa and MasterCard accepted

Linda West is one of a handful of mediums recommended by Allison DuBois from the TV series *Medium*.

Get a private reading with Linda:
Email: wingsoflight4477@yahoo.com
Website: www.lindawest-medium.com
Publicist and Media Events: Kathleen Malone
Kathleen@SundanceOnSuccess.com

MONEY AND MANIFESTING
by Dyan Garris

You think positive thoughts. You apply the law of attraction. You visualize. You even clear pathways to abundance. And you manifest nothing. Now you want to find out exactly what to do about it. You want wealth. You want prosperity. You want transformation. Here you will discover the real secrets to money and manifesting. What you learn will change your life forever.

Not just another manual about the laws of attraction and the power of positive thinking, Ms. Garris teaches what stands in our way of manifesting, how to unblock the energy flow of money, and how to actually transform energy to get what you desire.

Parts of the book are fictionalized. There is an intertwining story here that everyone can relate to. This helps your left brain integrate with your right brain. Integration is the foundation of manifestation. So, when you get done with the book you've already begun the first steps toward manifesting. Automatically.

"It is not enough to think positively, repeat affirmations, and attract positive energy. We must implement and integrate this learning into our daily lives. This is the real secret of manifesting money. It is the real secret to manifesting anything." -- Dyan Garris, author, New Age musician, and visionary mystic.

Angel Cards
by Dyan Garris

Voice of the Angels – A Healing Journey Spiritual Cards is a beautiful thirty card deck based on scenes from the guided fantasy, A Healing Journey, found on the companion CD of the same name. Each card has its own special channeled message in quatrain verse from the angels. The box of cards includes a 67 page instruction booklet showing twelve ways to lay out the cards, Transformational Healing Exercise, healing affirmations, and more. These cards were not computer drawn and therefore have different core energy than similar decks. Real crystals and gemstones were used to create the cards originally in 3D. Use for spiritual growth and transformation, divination, and connection to your angels.

Buy Dyan Garris products at www.voiceoftheangels.com, Amazon. com, and other retail outlets. Visit Voice of the Angels.com for the complete Spiritual Toolbox™, live psychic readings with real psychics, including renowned psychic medium Linda West, and free angel card readings online in three languages.

The Signature Collection
for Automatic Chakra Balance™
by Dyan Garris

Eight Chakra Balance Pendants
in Sterling Silver

Available at www.voiceoftheangels.com

"Wanted to let you know I received my chakra pendant #8. It is so very beautiful and I have worn it constantly since receiving it. I must say I feel such positive energy since I began wearing the pendant.....it is truly amazing!" – S. Marcus

Awakening of the Dream Riders
by Linda Louise Mangoro

This debut novel by Lynda Louise Mangoro is destined to be the next Harry Potter. "Awakening of the Dream Riders" is first in this new and promising series. This young teen metaphysical visionary fiction is hip, smart, edgy, and fun.

One day Kyra Sutton discovers she can fly. It's called "Dream Riding" and she's not the only one who can do it. But Dream Riding isn't about flying about in the physical body. It's about transcending the body and traveling in one's "light" body. Oh, the things they can do! These are kids with a mission. They are a completely new brand of superhero.

Contemporarily written, with an action packed plot, these characters come alive, literally jump off the page, and stick in your mind and heart. This story has it all and it's just the foundation for what is to come. Exciting and fresh.

Buy it now at Amazon.com

CPSIA information can be obtained at www.ICGtesting.com
Printed in the USA
LVOW081953140113

315673LV00001B/34/P